Re-Creating Schools

Re-Creating Schools

Places Where Everyone Learns and Likes It

Charles B. Myers
Douglas J. Simpson

CORWIN PRESS, INC.
A Sage Publications Company
Thousand Oaks, California

For information:

Corwin Press, Inc.
A Sage Publications Company
2455 Teller Road
Thousand Oaks, California 91320
E-mail: order@corwin.sagepub.com

SAGE Publications Ltd.
6 Bonhill Street
London EC2A 4PU
United Kingdom

SAGE Publications India Pvt. Ltd.
M-32 Market
Greater Kailash I
New Delhi 110 048 India

Printed in the United States of America

Library of Congress Cataloging-in-Publication Data

Myers, Charles B.
    Re-creating schools: Places where everyone learns and likes it /
by Charles B. Myers, Douglas J. Simpson.
        p.   cm.
    Includes bibliographical references and index.
    ISBN 0-8039-6426-9 (pbk.: acid-free paper). — ISBN 0-8039-6425-0
(cloth: acid-free paper)
        1. Educational change—United States. 2. Teaching—United States.
    3. Learning. 4. School management and organization—United States.
    5. Education—Aims and objectives—United States. I. Simpson,
    Douglas J. II. Title.
LA210.M94   1997
371.102—dc21   97-21224

This book is printed on acid-free paper.

98 99 00 01 02 03 10 9 8 7 6 5 4 3 2 1

Production Editor: Astrid Virding
Production Assistant: Lynn Miyata
Editorial Assistant: Kristen L. Gibson
Designer/Typesetter: Rebecca Evans
Cover Designer: Marcia M. Rosenburg

Contents

Preface

In this book, we propose a significantly different way of improving schools from current education reform, school restructuring, and university-school partnership efforts. We suggest that schools, and the learning and teaching that occur within them, be *re-created* by local school leaders and teachers who focus on their vision or visions of what their school culture, learning, and teaching would be like if all conditions were as they would like them to be. We also outline possible approaches to making this or similar visions real, and we describe standards for assessing progress along the way.

We believe that most current reform, restructuring, and partnership endeavors do not improve student learning and teaching as much and as quickly as is needed; we say this after many years of working in and studying these endeavors. Typically, the efforts concentrate on what is presently wrong with schools and try to fix the many parts, piece by piece. They devote much energy to changing people—primarily teachers—structures, and bureaucracies without affecting student learning in noticeable ways. We suggest that reformers look ahead to what schools, learning, and teaching *could* and *should be* rather than at what is not working.

Although the ideas we present here are based on insights and experiences of many other thinkers, practitioners, and writers as well as our own, we present them with a focus and a plan of action that combine grounded theories with specific and practical ways of implementing what we suggest. Even though we make it clear throughout the book that we see classroom teachers as the key actors in the process of making schools better, our target audiences are all who are

interested in improving schools, teaching, and student learning—
teachers, school leaders, parents, educational policy formulators,
teacher educators, and researchers. We speak especially to those who
are open to thinking about schools and school reform differently and
to acting on that thinking. Some of our colleagues have suggested that
the book changes the conversation about school reform. We hope that
it changes actions as well as conversation.

There are five chapters. Chapter 1, "Envisioning What Could Be,"
presents a case for the main point of the book—that we should look
toward new visions of what schools, teaching, and learning should be
as our destinations and guides as we re-create schools. It describes
briefly old myths about schools as factories and teaching as a craft and
explains why thinking of schools and teaching in these ways does not
help us create the schools we need. Then it sketches our suggested
four-dimensional alternative vision of schools and suggests how
teachers and school leaders can start the process of moving toward
this vision. The four dimensions of the proposed vision are:

- Schools as morally based communities of learners
- Learning as experience-based intellectual construction
- Teaching as a professional practice of investigative problem
  identification and problem solving
- Teacher learning as the development of professional knowl-
  edge, competence, and values in the context of practice

Each dimension is described briefly.

Chapter 2, "Revisioning Schools and Learning," describes and explains in some detail the first two dimensions of our suggested alternative vision of schools: Schools as morally based communities and
teaching as experience-based intellectual construction. It suggests
that schools be looked at as cultures and communities as anthropologists would look at them, and it stresses the importance of recognizing
(1) student learning as the unifying purpose and mission of schools,
(2) the premiere importance of teachers as professional experts and
primary school decision makers, and (3) the need for all participants
in a school community to create and maintain an authentic open atmosphere for everyone to be continuous, collegial learners. It then
describes learning as a three-element process in which all learners
use what they have already learned to interpret new ideas and experiences and, in the process, construct their personal understanding.

The chapter emphasizes that everyone is a learner all the time—teachers as well as students—and that the learning that occurs in schools is affected by experiences provided in the school community environment.

Chapter 3, "Revisioning Teaching and Professional Growth," explains the third and fourth dimensions of our suggested vision of schools on the horizon: teaching as a professional practice of problem identification and problem solving and teacher learning as the development of professional knowledge, competence, and values in the context of practice. It describes teachers as ever-learning professionals and schools as the centers where they do much of their learning. It suggests that the act of teaching be looked at as an investigative process in which teachers figure out how to help their students learn, try out what they think will work, assess the results, and reinvestigate. As teachers do this, they study teaching by inquiring into their own work along with their colleagues, by developing their own personal theories about their practice, and, in essence, by functioning as scholar practitioners. The chapter also describes the nature of teachers' professional knowledge, competence, and values in terms consistent with the ideas of constructivist learning as it is practiced by professional teachers in a context of a school community of learners. It explains how teachers acquire, develop, and use their professional knowledge, competence, and values for their teaching.

Chapter 4, "Getting There From Here," is the how-to-do-it chapter. It describes three elements in the process of making schools, teaching, and learning better: (1) formulating a clear image or vision of what any school would look like under ideal conditions, (2) assessing current local school conditions sincerely and honestly in comparison with that vision, and (3) journeying expeditiously and persistently from current circumstances to those envisioned for the school on the horizon. It cautions that the three-part task must be pursued locally by all participants of the school community and it must be led by teachers. It provides a comprehensive list of practical guiding questions, suggests what the journey is likely to look like, and offers three types of concrete examples of how to get started. It also stresses the importance of a positive attitude.

Chapter 5, "Monitoring, Assessing, and Celebrating," describes a way of assessing schools, teaching, and student learning that is consistent with the view of ideal schools that the book proposes. That way of assessing uses characteristics of ideal schools as criteria both for judging the quality of schools, teaching, and learning at any particular time and for judging the progress of school reform endeavors. The assessing process combines day-to-day monitoring with a comparison of current conditions against the ideal vision of how schools should be. Then it suggests and describes two sets of standards to use for defining how schools should be: those developed by local school community participants in terms of our proposed four-dimensional vision and those drawn from other present-day experts on assessing school quality. The chapter ends with specific guiding questions that can be used to answer the parallel questions, How can we know if we have a quality school? How can we know if our efforts to improve are succeeding?

We do not try to cover everything that educators need to understand to re-create schools. We simply suggest a different way of thinking about the task and we outline practical ways of implementing these ideas and assessing results. Because we believe that decisions about school reform need to be made by the school-level professionals who know local circumstances and have to carry out what is decided, we do not propose a tight formula to be followed by everyone, everywhere; instead, we present a sequence of guiding questions to be considered and decided on. Our questions and suggestions are positive ones. We are optimistic about what can be accomplished because we believe that re-creating schools, if tackled by sincere, informed practitioners, can be a successful and enjoyable experience—even though it is hard work.

We consciously decided not to devote much attention to the topic of change and we made that decision for two reasons: Doing so would detract from our focus on what can be accomplished, and many other authors have written well about the process of change.

We believe, however, that our suggestions have been guided by, and also describe ways of playing out, the following ideas about school and school change:

> When teachers work on personal vision-building and see how their commitment to making a difference in the classroom is connected to the wider purpose of education, it gives practical and moral meaning to their profession. When they pursue learning through constant inquiry, they are practicing what they preach, benefiting themselves and their students by always learning. . . .
>
> When many educators act this way, systems start to change, and become the environments that prod and support further growth and development. Independent change forces intersect to

produce radical breakthroughs. But it is not linear. The capacity to learn is as critical in facing setbacks as it is in celebrating successes. (Fullan, 1993, p. 145)

It's easier to design a new school culture than to change an existing one. And it's the whole school culture, not this or that program that stands in the way of learning. (Meier, 1997a, p. 9)

Cultivating thoughtful teaching calls for looking, listening, and feeling the school situation with respect for every point of view, and asking, again and again, what one small change we could try that is close to the heart of what matters most. (Clark, 1995, p. 142)

The fact is that no group knows more about the solutions that will work in our schools than America's teachers. We know what our schools need. (Chase, 1997)

Readers who are familiar with the literature on school reform will notice that we often draw on the insights of other thinkers and writers. Many of these thinkers have influenced our thinking significantly—they have helped us develop our ideas. We gratefully acknowledge that their ideas and writings have helped us enormously. We have been influenced especially by ideas expressed by Michael Eraut, Michael Fullan, Andy Hargreaves, Roland Barth, Thomas Sergiovanni, Seymour Sarason, Terrence Deal, John W. Gardner, and, of course, John Dewey.

We also want to acknowledge the suggestions and advice of our university and school colleagues in Nashville, Tennessee, and Fort Worth, Texas; fellow members of the Self-Study of Teacher Education Practices Special Interest Group of the American Educational Research Association; and colleague members of the American Association of Colleges for Teacher Education who have shared insights with us. We want to thank especially Lynn K. Myers, who helped develop the manuscript and to whom the book is dedicated; David Jones, who served as a research assistant and reviewer; Jeanne Woodward, who edited early drafts of several chapters; our Corwin editor, Alice Foster, who suggested we write the book; and Deloris Clark and Shellia Kirkendoll, who prepared the manuscript for production.

About the Authors

Charles B. Myers, PhD, is Professor in the Department of Teaching and Learning, Peabody College, Vanderbilt University, and Director of the Practice-based Professional Improvement Project with Metropolitan Nashville public schools, a project that is implementing many of the ideas presented in this book. He has held a number of leadership roles in the National Council for the Accreditation of Teacher Education and the National Council for the Social Studies. He is active in the American Association of Colleges for Teacher Education, the American Educational Research Association, and the International Society on Teacher Education. He teaches the beginning course for all Vanderbilt University teacher education undergraduate students and three doctoral-level courses for those studying for leadership roles in teacher education. He has written extensively in teacher education and is a consultant on school and program improvement. He has coauthored two texts for introductory education courses.

Douglas J. Simpson, PhD, is Professor in the Department of Educational Foundations and Administration, and Dean of the School of Education at Texas Christian University. He has been involved in numerous discussion, planning, and implementation groups to further equitable and reflective collaboration among school personnel and university professors. His major interests include the psychological and philosophical knowledge that is relevant to practicing teachers, counselors, and school psychologists as professionals. His current research interests include the roles and responsibilities of teachers and how these domains should affect the preparation and autonomy of educators. He has written extensively and has had several books published.

To Lynn K. Myers

CHAPTER ONE

Envisioning
What Could Be

*What visions of successful student learning and
quality teaching would serve as ideals if we were
to embark on a totally new journey to transform
schools?*

A mericans of the 1990s are noticeably disenchanted with their
schools and with what they perceive to be the lackluster efforts
of recent years to make those schools better. They believe that schools
should and can be improved but they do not know what improved
schools should look like and they have little faith that the many educational reform, school restructuring, and university-school partnership
efforts now underway will successfully create truly good schools. In
response to this dissatisfaction, few defend the status quo. Even those
directly involved with schools and with specific reform, restructuring,
and partnership endeavors do not claim to have answers that will
make significant differences in what schools do and achieve. Instead,
they devote their attention to correcting specific problems bit by bit
and case by case as best they can, while they explain how multifaceted and difficult the job of making schools better really is.

We understand this dissatisfaction and we agree that the tasks before us to make schools better are difficult. Both of us are and have
been involved in a number of specific reform efforts, and we believe
schools can be improved. But truly successful school improvement
requires different approaches to change from those of most current
education reform, school restructuring, and partnership efforts. As a
starting point, school improvement efforts should focus primarily not

1

on how schools are now and how each of their numerous problems should be addressed but on a positive vision of what schools could be like if reform efforts truly succeed. In essence, reforming schools requires a different way of thinking about schools and a different way of thinking about school change from that of the past, an alternative thinking that looks ahead toward a vision of schools that we describe as *learning communities*—cultural settings in which everyone learns, in which every individual is an integral part, and in which every participant is responsible for both the learning and the overall well-being of everyone else. In this book, we describe our vision of learning community schools—the way we think schools should be—and we suggest possible paths through which this vision can be realized.

Our vision of learning community schools has four overlapping dimensions: one dimension envisions schools as morally based cultural communities of learners, a second conceives of student learning as a process by which learners construct personal meaning from school-provided experiences, a third looks on teaching as professional problem identifying and problem solving, and a fourth describes teacher learning as career-long development of professional knowledge and competence. In the chapters ahead, we explain each of these dimensions in some detail and then we suggest possible ways in which they can be pursued.

 ## Rethinking Old Myths

For nearly the entire 20th century, two figures of speech—stated as either analogies or metaphors—have dominated much thinking about schools, learning, teaching, and teacher education. They are a major reason why reform, restructuring, and university-school partnerships have not been more successful in transforming education. These analogies and metaphors have hampered how current schools operate and how teaching is conducted, and they have made significant and substantial rethinking of schools, learning, teaching, and teacher education difficult. These analogies and metaphors are (1) schools are like factories and should be run by tight business-like management techniques; and (2) teaching is like a craft in which work is routine. In these analogies, workers do what supervisors tell them to do and new practitioners simply follow the practice of their more experienced masters.

Each figure of speech, whether stated as an analogy or a metaphor, greatly misinterprets schools, learning, and teaching. Together they have perpetuated educational hoaxes that are difficult to uproot and have served as bases for misdirected efforts to produce change (Darling-Hammond, 1990, 1993; Hawley, 1994).

1. *Schools as Factories*

The schools-as-factories metaphor became popular near the start of the 20th century and is embedded in the thinking about early industrialization in the United States. It probably never did fit schools, but whether it did or did not is not pertinent to our discussion. What is pertinent is that the metaphor does not fit schools today and it stifles attempts to make schools better (Tönnies, 1887/1957).

The schools-as-factories metaphor is antithetical to schools as learning communities because it accepts and reinforces at least two inappropriate premises about how schools function: (1) Schools are managed best by bureaucratically authorized experts, who know best how to educate students, to conduct classes, and to make schools work better; (2) The primary way to improve schools is to have hierarchically placed leaders decide what is best for individual schools and classrooms and then entice members of the school organization to implement those decisions. These two premises overlook the fact that children are not objects to be manipulated and mass produced and that teachers are not assembly line workers with only a few routine tasks to perform (Gibboney, 1994; Peters & Waterman, 1982; Prawat, 1993; Sergiovanni, 1992, 1994, 1996; Shedd & Bacharach, 1991).

2. *Teaching as a Craft*

The teaching-as-craft metaphor parallels the school-as-factories thinking. It is inappropriate because teaching requires much more than craft knowledge, is not routine (as most craft work is), and is not learned well by mirroring the expertise of masters. Teachers are confronted daily with unique teaching situations that they must handle according to their best professional judgments—monitoring and adjusting their actions every step of the way. Rather than being artisans, teachers must be knowledgeable, investigative, decision-making, executive managers. They manage subject matter content, class activities, student behavior, instructional resources, schedules, and much more. They investigate the learning needs of students and experiment in their efforts to meet those needs. They are the only ones who know enough about their individual students and classrooms to decide what to do, to try it, and to determine if it is working as well as it should be. Although they have much to learn, teachers are the only ones who know their teaching well enough to decide how to make it better (Berliner, 1990; Eraut, 1994; Lieberman & Miller, 1990b; Lortie, 1975, pp. 134-161; Prawat, 1993; Schön, 1987).

Teacher Motivation and Leadership

In his writing for school principals, Thomas Sergiovanni (1992) labels the style of school leadership that typically accompanies the school-as-factories and teaching-as-craft metaphors as the "expect and inspect" approach. He characterizes the approach by itemizing the following sequence of chores that administrators perform:

- State objectives.
- Decide what needs to be done to achieve these objectives.
- Translate these work requirements into role expectations.
- Communicate these expectations.
- Provide the necessary training.
- Put people to work.
- Monitor the work.
- Make corrections when needed.
- Practice human relations leadership to keep morale up.

Sergiovanni (1992) suggests that this factory-style leadership is derived from two types of authority: bureaucratic and psychological. In *bureaucratic authority*, a designated leader sets rules and regulations, formalizes job specifications, and gives explicit assignments. In *psychological authority*, a leader uses and manipulates rewards and incentives with workers, including teachers. Sergiovanni believes that good school leaders should avoid the old-style, bureaucratic management, rules-and-directives approaches with teachers in favor of the more subtle styles of enticement based on principles of psychology and group dynamics.

We find both approaches inappropriate for schools whose teachers are competent professionals. No matter how subtle or kind leaders' styles are, those who use either of the styles that Sergiovanni (1992) identifies assume that they know best what to do and think their role is to persuade teachers (who are assumed to be less knowledgeable) to do it—the factory and teaching-as-craft concepts are still guiding school operations and teachers are still being viewed as non-expert workers, not as professionals with expertise or as learners capable of developing professional expertise. Both types of authority assume that teachers are subordinates in the school's institutional hierarchy. Both expect teachers to follow orders from above without significant decision making on their part, even when those decisions concern what they believe is best for their classrooms and students (also see Barth, 1990; Lambert, Colay, Dietz, Kent, & Richert, 1997; Lambert, Walker, et al., 1995).

Fortunately, the factory, top-down, bureaucratic model is not very effective in penetrating beyond the closed classroom doors of good teachers, so most knowledgeable, thoughtful teachers make their own decisions and educate their students with little direct interference from school system bureaucratic rules and regulations (Jackson, 1986). Usually, however, they must do this by running against the bureaucratic tide instead of with the flow. This is counterproductive for them in at least two ways: (1) Running against the tide creates unnecessary anxiety for teachers and dissipates their energy, and (2) it fails to use effectively teacher expertise, power, influence, and commitment to the moral good they do.

One reason why the factory and craft models have not been discredited and discarded when applied to schools is that many teachers base what they do as professionals on their own expertise and simply ignore much that comes to them through the chain of command. This phenomenon has been the basis of several commercial films about exceptional teachers. Even students and the general public know that especially good teachers tend to do things their own way. Principals who know this stay out of the way of good teachers except to help them do what they do best.

Even though many schools and teachers succeed with students in spite of the schools-as-factories and teaching-as-craft models, the thinking hurts efforts to improve schools by denying teachers leadership roles in three ways. First, a business-style hierarchy puts teachers at the level of workers rather than of professional experts capable of making decisions about students, student learning, and how to teach. Second, this inappropriate hierarchy assumes that teachers need to be managed by technocrats, who hold supervisory places above them. Third, it relies on artificially constructed, extrinsic rewards to prompt teachers to teach better, instead of the intrinsic rewards inherent in teaching—a belief in the moral goodness of teaching, satisfaction in seeing students succeed and achieve, and personal feedback from students, colleagues, and parents that show appreciation for a job well done (Barth, 1988, 1990; Johnson, 1990; Lortie, 1975).

Rewarding teachers through the actions of hierarchically placed supervisors runs counter to studies on motivation in organizations in general (e.g., Herzberg, Mausner, & Snyderman, 1959) and seems to be particularly inappropriate for professional teachers, especially when school organizations are thought of as learning communities, as we suggest (e.g., Barth, 1990; Deming, 1982; Hachman, Oldham, Johnson, & Purdy, 1975; Johnson, 1990; Lambert et al., 1995, 1997; Little, 1992; Lortie, 1975; Prawat, 1993; Senge, 1990; Sergiovanni, 1992, 1996). These studies as a group reinforce several general points about teacher motivation.

One, good teachers are rewarded intrinsically by the work they do. Two, extrinsic, bureaucratic rewards are at best unnecessary and at worst demeaning and hinder good work. Three, those who want to encourage good teaching should devote their energies in two directions: (1) toward enhancing teacher opportunities to experience the rewards inherent in what they do rather than toward constructing external rewards, and (2) toward removing the hampering conditions of work that make the day-to-day tasks of teaching more difficult than they need to be. This last point is especially important. Teachers are not likely to experience the usual rewards of their work if they cannot succeed, if they believe the organization is unnecessarily burdensome, and if those whom they consider leaders are not helpful.

Why Current Reform, Restructuring, and Partnerships Are Not Enough

We are proposing alternative ways of thinking about schools and about school change because most current education reform, school restructuring, and university-school partnership endeavors have not and will not improve education—schools, student learning, teaching, and teacher learning—as much as most of us want and as much as is necessary for quality student learning. Many of these efforts do not challenge current views of schools, learning, teaching, and teacher learning as much as they should, and instead often accept present conceptualizations as being valid. At their worst, they blame the inadequate state of schooling on the officials who run the schools, the students who do the learning, and the teachers who do the teaching (e.g., Sarason, 1990, especially pp. 8-31). As a result of this thinking,

1. Reform, restructuring, and partnership efforts assume incorrectly that currently held ideas about the nature of schools and teaching are appropriate and that only the ways schools are organized and operate and the ways that teaching is conducted need changing.

2. The efforts undertaken in the name of significant change are essentially small-scale moves away from poor present conditions and practices instead of broad jumps toward something truly different and significantly better.

3. The efforts at change are encumbered by ideas, structures, and mechanisms of the past and present, often the very situations and circumstances that need to be replaced.

Asking the Wrong Questions

This old thinking asks questions such as, What is wrong with schools, student learning, teaching, and teacher education? What problems need correcting? How can we make what we now have better? Many of those who lead reform efforts use their answers to these questions as their guides as they push slowly along narrow paths, in linear fashion, and in small increments away from what is toward something slightly different and presumably slightly better. Their visions are significantly limited and their choices of what to do differently are inhibited by their desire to correct practices and conditions without making substantive changes. They focus on current operational problems and look over their shoulder at what they want to move away from, rather than looking ahead at what might be. They seem to want to assure themselves that, if their reform efforts make them too uncomfortable, they can always turn back.

Moving Away From What Is

As a result of this cautious attention to fixing current problems, visions of what could be are ignored or quickly forgotten as energies are narrowed to small-scale, short-term changes in how things are done. This is seen in the way success is reported in reform, restructuring, and partnership movements.

For example, many reformers and university-school collaborators set out to transform both schools and teacher education into entities known as professional development schools, but they report successes not in terms of changed schools, improved student learning, better teaching, and qualitatively improved teacher education but in terms of the number of college professors who visit school classrooms or the forming of university-school collaborative committees, which they hope may some day improve or alter both student and teacher learning.

Similar success reporting is used by many school restructurers in their work to transform schools into participatory learning communities. They note their success not by citing improved student learning and a more professional school culture but by describing the forming of site-based management teams and by counting the times when the school principal chooses to allow teachers and parents to make specific decisions formerly reserved for the principal (assuming, of course, that the principal holds on to the real power; e.g., Harris, 1992).

It seems to us that these reform, restructuring, and partnership endeavors appear to parallel in two ways a family's first-ever vacation trip to a picturesque lake in the country. The family is motivated initially more by a desire to get away from the burdens of normal life than by the attraction of the vacation, but as they anticipate the trip, family members gradually develop an attractive image of a dream vacation. They do not really know what the vacation will be like because they have not yet had the experience, so all they can do is gather information and recollect past experiences that they think are relevant and then make some inferences.

These inferences reflect more of the conditions they want to escape from than foreshadow the actual experiences family members will confront at the lake. If the hassles leading to the trip are typical, the process of reaching the dream will be so transformed by the burdens that preceded it—running last-minute errands, closing the house, getting away from work, packing the car, and driving through traffic—that a quiet first night in a motel at the edge of the city may easily substitute for the anticipated first evening by the lake. After all, the family is away from home and work.

As long as the night at the motel is only a necessary stopping point in the process of getting to the lake, the dream of the vacation remains in family members' minds, even if somewhat diminished. But if the challenges of reaching the lake become too burdensome, the family might give up the dream and become satisfied with a stay at the motel.

The motivations and experiences of some education reformers, school restructurers, and university-school partners parallel the family. For example, when many schools leaders set out to improve school climates and student learning through site-based management, they have to devote much attention to the mechanics of change and restructuring how decisions are made and who makes them. For at least a time, the mechanics of the change and restructuring become the task instead of an improved climate and learning. If those leaders are not both careful and persistent in reaching the original goal, setting up the site-based arrangements becomes the new goals and improved school climate and student learning fade into the distance.

This phenomenon occurs, at least in part, because leaders' ideas of what to expect are more tied to the past than to the future and their visions of the future do not create adequate images of what education could be like if their endeavors succeed. Also, as they pursue their limited efforts, they confuse their visions and goals with the means they use to attain them and they substitute new procedures and small changes in current practice for original dreams. Their means are quickly substituted for ends.

The very terms *reform, restructure,* and *partnership* assume starting with what is and changing it, not starting with images of something truly different and building toward them. All three terms as used by many educators also seem to imply a change process that is linear, incremental, predictable, controllable, and not particularly uncomfortable. This thinking leads to the educational equivalent of Jurassic Park. When more things change than are predicted, those affected panic, hunker down, and back up (Hargreaves, 1994).

A Need for New Questions

It is time to begin asking more fundamental questions—questions such as, How should we rethink schools, learning, and teaching? What would each of these look like if all conditions were imaginatively and thoughtfully developed? What would each look like if we were to create them from scratch? What are our greatest attainable goals? How would we design our instruction if we could create desirable learning environments?

Substantive questions such as these that are framed in terms of forward-looking visions will yield results better than past attempts to avoid dissatisfying conditions. These questions can help us identify more deeply what we expect of schools, teaching, and teacher learning and can challenge more persistently the ideas and assumptions that have led to current school practices, structures, and conditions.

For education to be what it needs to be, we must be guided by truly different visions of what could be rather than by more easily understood, shorter-term, and more manageable goals of making what is now in place better. What is required is a *rethinking* that leads to a *re-creation* beyond reform, restructuring, or partnering. The thinking must break from the past and present, and the visions and subsequent goals must be distinct from the processes involved in attaining them. The visions must serve as ideals that guide the change effort, whereas the processes provide the path. Mileposts along the path might mark intermediate accomplishments, but they cannot substitute for the envisioned goals. Of course, means-level activities will often stimulate a rethinking of schools and teacher learning and that rethinking may change the final vision.

This is not to say that those who want to change education can ignore the present, develop radically new ways of doing things without proceeding in increments, or achieve their vision of education without much trial and error. But there must be new visions; visions that those seeking them can distinguish, at least in part, from the means of achieving them. As we look to education in the future, questions such as the following need to serve as beacons:

- What are the central purposes of schools and how can these purposes be better served?
- What constitutes student learning and how can it be nurtured by teachers?
- What is good teaching and what does it look like in practice?
- How can teacher education be of greater and better help to schools, teachers, and students? (Barth 1990; Lambert et al., 1995, 1997)

In the analogy of the vacationing family, its members, as they seek a vacation at the picturesque lake, actually want more than to get away. They want to experience a dream vacation even if they do not really know what to expect. They probably anticipate the hassles, but they put up with them to make the trip. They know that getting to the lake involves a different set of experiences from the experience of being there. They probably do not confuse the dream with reality or the means with the goal. And their image of the anticipated vacation is a force that makes the burden of getting there acceptable. The dream involves much more than just getting away from work and the neighborhood for a few days. It includes an attraction to what is ahead, not just a push from what is being left behind.

Similarly, those who set out to reform school climates and noticeably improve student learning truly want to accomplish their mission, reach their dream, even if the dream is only a vague image in the distance. But the dream, image, mission must remain ever before them as a destination and a guide—as the way schools and learning should be, and will be when all the hard work succeeds.

 ## Reform, Restructuring, and Partnership Endeavors as Starting Points

Although current reform, restructuring, and partnership endeavors by themselves are not likely to create the kinds of school improvement needed to develop learning community schools, most can play important roles in moving us in that direction. They can serve as first steps toward more thorough conceptual shifts in our thinking about the nature of schools and all that occurs in and around them. As first steps, they can lead us toward improved learning, teaching, and teacher learning and they can start action that can be built on (Sarason, 1990).

Those of us who want to build learning community schools have to begin somewhere. We cannot stop the way in which schools, learning, teaching, and teacher education currently occur and start all over again. We must find appropriate situations and circumstances in the educational enterprise that can become (1) *points of intrusion* into current practice—points at which what is currently happening can be interrupted so a new direction can be pursued, (2) *places of departure* from current practice toward a new vision—platforms from which the new endeavor can be launched, and (3) *vehicles* for moving us toward the vision—efforts that carry us from where we are to where we should be (Myers, 1979, 1981, 1996b).

Points of Intrusion

These points of intrusion or convenient places to interrupt consist of times, events, and activities in schools and teaching that can be used to initiate experimentation, prompt new thinking, and test the efficacy of new ideas and new ways of doing things—that show whether they produce better student learning or not. For example, they might occur when teachers are dissatisfied or bored with the way things are, when new curriculum materials are being adopted, when new technology is being purchased, when a new principal is being selected, when new teachers are hired, when a cluster of teachers is willing to experiment in any way, and when universities want to reconsider teacher preparation with school-based practitioners.

Places of Departure

Although potential points of intrusion are plentiful, those that prompt substantial and long-term change must be carefully selected from among current school situations and events so that they can also serve as appropriate places of departure, that is, so they can provide conditions or circumstances that will do more than produce single, small-scale change, ones that will stimulate rethinking and will bring about the fashioning of different images of schools, learning, teaching, and teacher education. As places of departure, they need to produce more than one new way of doing things. They need to launch a long sequence of changes and improvements, and they need to provide contexts that sustain continual and substantial rethinking. An example is a curriculum revision effort that involves a year-long analysis by teachers of their teaching methods instead of an every-5-year adoption of a new text series.

Vehicles for Change

Each activity that is undertaken in the name of school improvement must do more than launch change, however. It must also serve as a vehicle for change that continues into the future, that is, it must provide the means by which each change is sustained, always generating more change, rippling out in ever-broader ways. These vehicles must be able to carry into the school community environment both a norm for and a commitment to continuing change and improvement. For example, once teachers start the analysis of their teaching methods, they can build that type of analysis into their regular roles as teachers and it can become a part of what the teachers expect of themselves as they teach.

These points of intrusion, places of departure, and vehicles for change can be quite varied. They are, in fact, present all the time in the normal operations of schools and the day-to-day work of teachers. The challenge to using them effectively is recognizing them and making the most of the opportunity. They might be small in scale, affecting only a few teachers, or schoolwide or larger, but the changes that grow from them must involve the whole school community; must trigger rethinking, not just one-shot changes; and must establish continuous renewal as a sustainable norm.

Although we acknowledge that many current reform and restructuring efforts, including a number of university-school partnerships, are superficial, artificial, and ineffective and that some that start with good intentions lack vision and fail to make meaningful progress, many reform efforts, especially professional development schools (PDSs) that include teacher educators, provide potentially appropriate points of intrusion, places of departure, and vehicles for change, and they do so for several reasons.

First, most partnerships and PDSs were established for the stated purposes of making large-scale and long-term changes in practice and for rethinking schools, teacher education, and the process of change in general.)

Second, many of these larger efforts attempt to draw together a range of professional educators who need to work in concert more often and more effectively if schools, learning, teaching, and teacher education are to be rethought and made better. Typically, good broad-scale PDSs include teachers, school administrators, policy specialists, teacher educators, educational researchers, and theoretical scholars, and they focus on places in the education enterprise at which these role players' expertise and interests intersect. In contrast, most other types of reform efforts have more narrowly identified focuses and constituents, and their key actors seem to have less time and motivation to engage in serious self-analysis and to seek ideas and advice from those undertaking parallel efforts at change outside their immediate purview.

Third, larger efforts attempt wide ranges of changes, each of which has multiple effects on the education enterprise in general and, therefore, creates the opportunity and need for additional changes.) If these rippling effects are encouraged and directed appropriately, change can build on change and, eventually, change can become a consistent and accepted cultural norm. If this happens, the reform activities serve not only as points of intrusion into what is but also as places of departure toward what can be and vehicles for getting there.

Fourth, the multiple activities of establishing, operationalizing, and conducting larger reform efforts serve as optimal vehicles for change because they require so many concomitant changes in how schools, learning, teaching, and teacher education are conducted.) Even those who become involved only peripherally often have to replace some of what they have been doing with new ways and have to think differently about what they do. In effect, the new ways force change in the thinking of even those who got involved without understanding what their involvement meant or got involved only reluctantly and for the wrong reasons. As they evolve, these efforts force participants to make unanticipated changes that they would not have chosen to make if they had been asked to do so at the start.

We do not mean to suggest that most current large-scale reform and restructuring efforts pursue the vision of learning community schools that should be our guide for creating the kind of schools we need. In fact we know of none that do, and that is why our suggested vision of schools as learning communities transcends most current thinking and practice. Broad-scale reform efforts offer appropriate places to start, however.

Reforms That Can Be Built On

Even the fact that most current reform efforts are not by themselves adequate vehicles for change can be a useful point of departure in a seemingly negative way. Their approaches to change and many of their specific ways of trying to produce change can be beginning points that are adequate at first and noticeably inadequate as they evolve to the point at which sustained change and reconceptualizing schools, learning, and teaching are necessary. For example, many shifts to block scheduling in high schools change the daily lives of all involved, but sooner or later questions are asked such as, How has the learning of students improved? Often the answer is disappointing. Because such endeavors start change and experimentation but soon stall, they become imperfect examples of reform, which can be improved on as the change process progresses. Questions can be asked such as what more do we need to do?

A closer look at PDS partnerships can serve as an example. Many current PDSs attempt inappropriately to make things better (1) by imposing changes by force from outside, (2) by placing too many and contradictory demands on teachers, (3) by focusing on what is (usually the weakest aspects of what is) rather than on what could be, and (4) by pursuing single-step efforts away from what is toward narrow conceptions of something better (Myers, 1995a, 1996a, 1996b, 1997b). All these attempts can start a change process but, if not modified, they are not likely to create significantly improved teaching or student learning. They break from past practices and arrangements, but where they lead is often unsatisfying.

When those involved in these efforts realize the inadequacy of what is happening, however, they can make adjustments that can be successful. They can see that, although there is little evidence that the goals of improved teaching and learning are being attained, there is clear evidence that the first stages of reform are under way. They will see some progress and will know that it is time to revise their expectations and pursue appropriate next steps. If they are sincere about their goals, they will push on toward a higher level of change for what they now understand to be the long haul.

Similar imperfect examples of real change come from reform and restructuring efforts whether they are parts of PDS endeavors or not. For instance, in many school restructuring efforts, administrators push interdisciplinary teaching and block scheduling without attending to the requisite teacher development needs for those plans to work and without enough attention to how and if the efforts will improve teaching or student learning. Policymakers often impose stringent academic accountability standards in basic subjects on teachers at the same time that they add expectations for teaching additional subject matter such as sex education, HIV-AIDS education, and counterviolence education; and they thrust on teachers additional classroom responsibilities such as the full inclusion of severely disabled students. Frequently, the teachers on whom these responsibilities are placed are not provided with the necessary instruction or support. Similarly, teacher education reformers replace semester-long student teaching with year-long internships but change little else. Others assign campus-based higher education faculty to weekly visits to pre-K-12 schools with little attention to what the visits should accomplish in terms of better student learning or teaching.

When seemingly strong reform, restructuring, and PDS endeavors bog down in a confusion of means and goals, they can also serve as imperfect examples of reform that can be improved on. As they bog down, they send warning signals that something is wrong and require greater efforts to overcome the unforeseen challenges, and they provide illustrations of circumstances that other reform efforts should avoid or push beyond. For example, when the direct involvement of college faculty in pre-K-12 schools and the establishment of site-based management committees begin to be thought of by those involved as goals rather than as means toward the bigger goals of improved teaching and student learning, the error is in the thinking, not in the activities. As soon as the college faculty placement in schools and the forming of the site-based committees are rethought of as first steps instead of goals, the reform process can regenerate and move on.

If typical reform, restructuring, and PDS efforts are to serve as both places of departure and vehicles for change, that opportunity comes when those involved realize that their efforts are not resulting in enough change to improve teaching and learning. This time of realization is critical because it presents the dilemma of the proverbial fork in the road, but this time there are three choices. The reformers can back off and return to the old ways of doing things: "We already tried it. It doesn't work." They can substitute means for goals: "Even if the students are not learning better, our teachers are doing whole language." "Even if our graduates do not demonstrate that they are noticeably better teachers, they are in real classrooms much longer during their internship." Or they can pause, rethink, and make more substantial conceptual changes: "If this isn't accomplishing what we had hoped, what is absent from our thinking and how can we make what we are doing better?" If they opt for the third choice, their initial efforts at reform, restructuring, and partnership formation can eventually lead to real change (Fullan, 1993).

An Alternative Vision

We suggest an alternative vision of what schools could be as a guide for us as we rethink and re-create schools. We call the vision a *learning community school.* The vision has four dimensions; each dimension describes a different way of looking at four traditional components of schooling: the school as an organization, student learning, teaching, and teacher education. Our views of the four dimensions are presented in general terms on the next few pages and explained in more detail in Chapters 2 and 3.

Schools as Morally Based Communities of Learners

When schools are thought of as the learning communities that we envision, they are cultures rather than physical locations, buildings, organizations, institutions, places where students and teachers congregate, or clusters of employees who work together. As cultures, they have a moral purpose, a mission, and a shared set of core values. Their moral purpose is to educate students and their central goal is all students learning at the highest possible levels. These are, of course, the commonly recognized mission and central goals of all schools, but in learning community cultures, the mission and goal are recognized constantly and more forcefully and both are used more consistently to create better learning for all.

In these ideal learning communities, all community members—students, teachers, school staff, and parents—possess a sincere commitment to achieving the mission and believe in the core values noticeably, sincerely, and deeply. The scene might be equated to a farm or ranch that is owned and operated by all the members of a large extended family—parents, children, aunts, uncles, cousins all work together, live together, and pursue a common set of goals. In comparable school communities, each member belongs to the community and is wanted by all other members. All members possess senses of loyalty, camaraderie, and collegiality that draw everyone into a common bond. Attachments to the community, to one another, and to the mission are so strong that they supersede attachments to individual personal desires and are conceived of in ways that assure that everyone helps each other toward both common and personal goals. The shared mission and common beliefs in core community values permeate every aspect of school life and guide all school decisions and activities. Learning is celebrated and is everyone's responsibility.

Learning as Experience-Based Intellectual Construction

When learning is viewed in terms of our vision, it is conceptualized as a three-part intellectual process by which learners (1) gain ideas from new learning experiences, (2) match these ideas with what they have already learned, and (3) construct their own personal meaning, develop their own competence, and formulate their own values (Myers, 1997b). Students learn because of the experiences that teachers make possible, rather than because of something specific that teachers impart. In short, learning is what learners do. This process is described by John Holt, when he writes about playing the cello and learning to play the cello in an excerpt printed in *Chicken Soup for the Soul* (Canfield & Hansen, 1993). Holt points out that people who comment to him about his playing the cello often divide (1) his learning to play the cello and (2) his playing the cello into two separate processes, as if someone learns to do something to a point and then stops learning and does it. Holt calls this separation between learning and doing nonsense: "There are not two processes, but one. We learn to do something by doing it. There is no other way" (p. 132).

With this image of learning, students come to be thought of as community members who experience learning in a way that is similar to participating in summer camp, in a concert orchestra, on an athletic team, or at an audience-involving play production. Students learn from their participation in school experiences rather than merely from absorbing sets of ideas, skills, or value perspectives that their teachers present to them.

For this kind of learning to happen, teachers need to create learning experiences for students rather than produce a particular school product, and they need to ensure that all students participate in educative activities. In fact, the learning experiences that they create need to be available to and engaged in by a wide array of community members—themselves, school staff members, and parents, as well as students. In a learning community, everyone experiences learning all the time (Barth, 1990; Beck & Murphy, 1996; Eisner, 1992; Lambert et al., 1995, 1997; Newman & Wehlage, 1995; Noddings, 1992; Schlechty, 1990; Slater, 1996; Wasley, 1993).

Teaching as Investigative Problem Identification and Problem Solving

When teaching is seen through the lenses that we suggest, it becomes a career-long process of investigative problem identification and problem solving, a process that starts when future teachers are still classroom students and does not stop before retirement, if it stops then. The process combines learning to teach and doing teaching into one common professional endeavor, and it is as continuous as John Holt's efforts to learn to play the cello.

When viewed as investigative problem identification and problem solving, teaching consists of two successive tasks: (1) figuring out ways to educate the students for whom one is responsible, and (2) trying these ideas in the classroom. When the problem solving is successful, students learn. When it is not, teachers reassess and try to solve the problem again. For example, teachers give diagnostic tests, decide based on the test results how to provide the learning that individual students need, try the plan, reassess, replan, and so on.

Teaching That Includes Construction of Professional Knowledge, Skills, and Values

As problem identification and problem solving, teaching can be seen as a professional intellectual investigation in which teachers construct new professional knowledge, refine professional skills, and sort out professional value perspectives. Teachers come to understand, more clearly than most now do, that they do not learn to teach simply by receiving information from others or by replicating the teaching that they have experienced or observed. They *construct* their own professional knowledge, skills, and value perspectives by drawing on all their life experiences and formulating from them their own unique professional ways of understanding and doing things. They go beyond teaching the ways their teachers taught them or the ways their college professors told them to teach. They study, but they move beyond the ideas they read about. They also look at their own practice; analyze, reflect on, and ponder about what they do in their own classrooms; they build the ideas they learn from this self-study into their own professional theories. Then they use these personally constructed theories for future practice, continually revising and building toward better teaching and better student learning. Because teaching is investigative, teachers draw from research-based theory, from what they read and hear, from the examples of others, and from their own experimental efforts. In the process, they select ideas and examples from others' good practice for their classrooms, not as if the work of others serves as exemplars to be adopted uncritically but as information from which to form their own personal professional judgments to construct their own professional practice (Dewey, 1916/1944, 1938/1963; Lambert et al., 1995, 1997; Vygotsky, 1962, 1978).

Teaching as Complex, Continuous, Individual Investigation

In our view, teaching is too complex and too tied to the unique circumstances and individuals in a particular classroom to be thought of as a craft that can be learned primarily on a college campus or in summer or after-school workshops and then applied through a relatively short period of guided practice called student teaching, internship, or implementation. It is not something learned at the start of a professional career and then repeated for 25 to 30 years. It is also not something done according to prescriptions handed down by school administrators, supervisors, curriculum committees, textbook authors, or outsiders who develop packaged programs.

Teaching as investigative problem identification and problem solving is, instead, a multifaceted endeavor. It joins theory and practice, research and implementation, and preservice and in-service teacher learning. It avoids dividing teachers into novice-expert categories. Instead, it acknowledges a developmental continuum through teachers' professional careers. This sort of teaching cannot be prescribed. Instead, it is a set of complex understandings and judgments that each teacher builds personally and then uses when interacting with a learner.

When teaching is conceived of as investigative problem identification and problem solving, teachers are seen by all as the primary experts in schools, and their work is seen as the most prized thing schools do. All other participants in the school community—administrators, other staff members, and parents—become primarily their support.

When teaching is understood in these ways, teachers make learning a part of their every day lives; they use that learning in their future work. The process continues for as long as they teach. It is both guided and driven by constantly asked questions: How can I teach better? How can I create better educative experience for students? Similarly, the work of every other professional in the school community, including those in administrative and supervisory positions, is guided by parallel questions: How can I help teachers teach better? How can I create a more educationally supportive environment? Once teaching is viewed as a career-long process of professional investigation and problem solving in which teachers continuously construct their own professional knowledge, one's views of both teacher learning and what teachers do to teach become much clearer. We begin to see the learning as cumulative and personally formulated in the context of professional work. We also begin to see teacher knowledge as that which is personally formulated in that same context. In the next section of this chapter, we refer to that knowledge as the *knowledge of practice.*

Professional Knowledge as the Knowledge of Practice

When the professional knowledge, competence, and value perspectives that teachers need to possess are thought of as described above, that knowledge, that competence, and those values are conceptualized as knowledge personally constructed, competence personally developed, and value perspectives personally formulated by teachers in the context of their professional work. The conceptualization includes at least four commingled elements, the first of which we have already mentioned:

- Teachers construct knowledge, skills, and values rather than merely absorb them.
- Teachers validate their knowledge, skills, and values by testing their usefulness.
- Teachers learn from teaching, sometimes formulating personal, practical theories that they use in subsequent teaching.
- Teachers never stop learning, thinking, and changing (see Eraut, 1994).

Each element is elaborated on below.

Professional Learning as Intellectual Construction

In ways consistent with our previously stated descriptions of both learning and teaching, teachers construct professional knowledge, skills, and values themselves rather than merely absorb them from lectures, workshops, readings, and other external sources. Admittedly, teachers gather information from numerous sources—college professors, textbooks, cooperating teachers, consultants, research studies, the practices of colleagues, and their own experiences as students. But from all these they construct and develop their own unique ways of knowing, doing things, and believing based on their own background and experience. For example, teachers who attend a particular workshop demonstration might leave enthused, cynical, or unaffected by what they see and hear based in the experience, knowledge, and attitude they bring to the setting. On the other hand, however, teachers—as members of learning communities—are not isolated entities. They are accountable for what they think, believe, and practice. They are responsible to the profession, their students, and society to base their beliefs and behaviors on sound reasoning and relevant evidence. In short, their practice must be ethically and pedagogically defensible.

Validation by Usefulness

Teachers validate their knowledge, skills, and values by testing their usefulness. They ask themselves, for example, how the information they are told in a lecture or the skill they see another teacher demonstrate will fit with their own ways of doing things and how it will work with their own students and in their own classrooms. They ask, can I teach my present students this way? Am I up to the task? Will Jane and Adam get it? What will I do if they do not?

The ways in which they answer these types of questions not only affect how and if they use the knowledge, they also transform the very nature of that knowledge. The same point applies to skills and values. This transformation of knowledge, skills, and values happens because teachers determine the validity of ideas and the appropriateness of skills and value perspectives differently from the ways in which the validity and appropriateness are typically assessed by college teacher educators, administrators, and policy specialists. For classroom teachers, the validation comes in terms of how well their own students learn and for what purpose they learn. Because of the need for this type of experiential validation, the value of any set of professional knowledge, skills, and value perspectives, as far as teachers are concerned, is determined by its use in helping individual teachers teach rather than by its scholarly origin. The reputation of the developer (whether central office staff, independent consultant, or university professor) of a recommended teaching procedure and the sophistication of the research project in which it was developed do not outweigh the teacher's belief, after reflective trial in his or her classroom, that it helps specific students learn particular ideas, skills, or values. The teacher as a reflective professional is the final arbiter of good practice in individual learning situations (Eraut, 1994).

Formulating Personal, Practice-Based Theories

The places that teachers turn to as sources of knowledge, skills, and values are not all external to themselves and their classrooms. Teachers generate their own educational theories from their teaching, reflection on that teaching, and self-analysis. They test and refine their theories on a daily basis. They plan a lesson, teach it, decide if it worked, and consider if they should add it to their repertoire or not. Each day they teach, they learn from what they try, how it works, how students respond, the social context in which it takes place, how they assess all this, and so forth. This learning from practice simply happens as a normal part of teaching. When it works well, teachers formulate their in-class learning into personal, practical theories that they use in subsequent teaching. They communicate these theories to other teachers and, in turn, they use in their classrooms similar theories developed by their colleagues. Together they and their colleagues mature as a learning community that keeps using prior and present learning (Clandinin & Connelly, 1987, 1995; Lambert et al., 1995, 1997; Schön, 1983, 1987).

Continuous Professional Learning

Because teachers are adults and continuously developing professionals, they never stop learning. At any given time in their individual careers, teachers possess ideas, competencies, and value perspectives different from those they possessed a short time earlier or will possess a short time in the future. They, like all humans, never stop thinking and changing (Leithwood, 1992). This is not to say that all teachers are always growing. Obviously, some do not learn as much as they should. Others back-slide from their sound practices. They forget, lose proficiency, and narrow their perspective. A vibrant professional learning community provides protection against these possibilities, however.

When teaching is thought of as professional practice, the knowledge, skills, and values that teachers possess and use in their work to cultivate learning are not limited to preservice professional education; craft knowledge passed on by master craftspersons; that which is absorbed from books, lectures, workshops, and research reports; or individual teacher experiments guided by reflective judgment. The knowledge, skills, and values are developed from all the above and other sources too, such as students, parents, and colleagues. In this way of seeing things, teaching, studying teaching, and educating teachers are three facets of the same enterprise, not three separate endeavors to be conducted independently by teachers, researchers, and teacher educators.

A Context of Interconnectedness

We acknowledge that our ideas about the nature of schools, learning, teaching, and teacher professional knowledge and competence are not new, and they are readily available for anyone interested in changing or re-creating schools and teacher preparation; they are available to use as guides in the work of developing different kinds of institutions and teacher education programs. They are scattered across contemporary scholarly literature in many specific areas of study, including education reform, school restructuring, organizational cultures, institutional leadership, the nature of knowledge, the nature of learning, teaching effectiveness, adult learning, and reflective practice.

Isolated Reforms

For the most part, the ideas in each of these areas of study, as well as those in many other domains, seem to be pursued by most reformers in relative isolation from each other; when reformers are attracted to specific ideas, they seem to apply them to educational practice either as single innovations or as one-shot solutions for particular problems. These isolated approaches to reform ignore both the interconnectedness of the various facets of educational practice and the continuous nature of educational change. For example, most reform proposals of recent years concerning teaching effectiveness and accountability overlook research information about organizational communities and impose in top-down fashion procedures and accountability standards that experts who study institutional leadership reject as unworkable. Similarly, many school restructuring and university-school partnership proposals tend to ignore the latest thinking about the construction of knowledge, professional development, and adult learning.

A Separation Between Research and Practice

A similar lack of connection exists between researchers who develop ideas for improving education and teachers who are expected to put the ideas into practice. For instance, many of those who study teaching and recommend change concentrate their energies on formulating theories without knowing whether their findings can be applied in a particular school context. Although there are noticeable exceptions, those who generate research-based theory tend to see research and practice as a one-way, theory-to-practice flow, and they often deny any personal responsibility for testing their theories or applying their findings in actual classrooms. Moreover, they sometimes denigrate theory developed from classroom practice much as some practitioners denigrate theory developed by research. To illustrate, researchers who study constructivist learning fail to connect professionally with teacher educators and curriculum specialists (who teach teachers about constructivism even though their understanding of the subject is second hand and superficial). Because of this disconnectedness, many who instruct teachers approach the implementation process mechanistically and teach in nonconstructivist, didactic ways.

The Need for Connecting

Although there are many good ideas about making the education enterprise better, few will become common practice unless educators become more successful than they have been at creating profound changes in school and classroom practice. To do this, they need to develop a philosophy of education that enables them (1) to develop sound, compatible ideas, and (2) to try a select few in the classroom. In the process, they must realize that these ideas will be transformed as they are tried in real schools and classrooms—as they are constructed and reconstructed in the minds and work of teachers. In effect, each idea about how to improve or re-create education must be abstracted from one context and rebuilt in the new settings in which it is being tried. In addition, the innovations must be seen by teaching practitioners as useful new ways of doing things, and these new ways must result in improved student learning.

Some disconnectedness is only natural. It is understandable that all educational researchers must focus on specific areas of study; they cannot investigate everything simultaneously or change everything at once. Their expertise and interests are limited. They do not know enough to study all facets of teaching, learning, and schools, and if they did, an attempt to improve all areas at one time for all teachers and all students would be foolhardy. Researchers, reformers, and implementors have to devote their attention to doable tasks and pursue changing some aspects of the education enterprise while other areas remain relatively stable. So they specialize and try to fix one or a few things at a time.

Nevertheless, those trying to change the education enterprise need to understand how interconnected their work is and realize that making the changes needed involves more than a number of individual, parallel, linear processes. They must also see the broader context—of present day schools, learning, teaching, and teacher education—not as static phenomena set at fixed points in time from which they can be moved forward rather simplistically, but as multiple parts of a mammoth enterprise floating on a sea of constant change.

Because the tasks before us involve so many ideas, so many different players, so many aspects of the education enterprise, and so many specific settings, and because we can figure out better ways of doing things only while schools, teaching, and teacher education continue to function (we cannot stop everything and start over), many of us see the task ahead as unbelievably complicated, often incomprehensible, messy, and unnerving. This explains why technical-rational, administrator-imposed, top-down ways of changing schools, with their well-stated objectives and precise predeveloped plans for others to implement, have not served us well. Neither have centrally formulated strategic plans in general. (Sometimes it seems a more useful guide would be something closer to chaos theory.) We cannot all march in the same direction toward predictable ends if we are to preserve professional judgment for contextually different learning communities. Even so, as we experiment with separate reform agendas, we should stay informed of others' work, continue to educate ourselves along the way, and appreciate the magnitude of the general effort. When we need encouragement to sustain us along the way, we can rationalize by saying, "If the tasks of making schools, learning, teaching, and teacher education better were easier than they are, we would have been more successful by now."

The four dimensions of the vision that we have outlined—(1) the moral community nature of schools, (2) the constructivist nature of learning, (3) the problem-identification and problem-solving nature of teaching, and (4) the personally constructed nature of teacher knowledge and competence—allow us to consider the many facets of school improvement in an interconnected, forward-looking context. The dimensions and the vision as a whole can provide direction for reformers, restructurers, and university-school collaborators, as well as for a general coherent reform movement. They can help us decide where we want to go and how to get there. They can also help reformers—researchers and teachers—see the importance of interacting with and informing each other and see the value of being guided by ideas that are, at a minimum, compatible.

CHAPTER TWO

Revisioning Schools and Learning

*How should we describe life and learning
in a learning community school?*

For the learning community schools that we envision to develop, our thinking about schools, student learning, teaching, and teacher education needs to be different from that of the past. It needs to be more visionary—more forward looking, more able to interconnect the various elements of education reform, and more capable of guiding us as we re-create schools as they should be. In Chapter 1, we outline four dimensions of our alternative vision for schools. In this chapter, we describe two of these dimensions in more detail—those concerning the nature of schools and the nature of learning. Two other dimensions—those concerning teaching and teacher learning—are described in Chapter 3.

 ## Schools as Morally Based Learning Communities

Schools are unique and special entities. They are more than places, buildings, and organizations where learning happens. They are centers where educational experiences are created for children and youth who are in transition as they evolve from the narrow, protective environments of their family and neighborhood to broader, more exposed environments of the world at large. These experiences enable young people to mature as human beings. They help them construct ideas, develop competencies, and formulate values. The schools where these experiences occur, if they are good schools, are communities of people rather than geographic locations, and those communities include professionals responsible for developing students' habits of mind and habits of heart.

Schools, as these special entities, can be thought of and explained in terms of the purposes for which they were founded, what they attempt to accomplish, and who they serve. They exist to do good and important work, to educate the children and youth of a society, and thereby to improve society itself. Their reason for being is, therefore, a moral one. As cultures, their moral purposes are unmatched by other institutions in our society.

To arrive at our vision of learning community schools, we start with two basic beliefs: (1) schools should be communities whose central mission is to educate students, and (2) that mission is morally good in and of itself and, as a consequence, needs no other justification. Because of these beliefs, we think that all who wish to create better schools should strive to develop true learning communities— schools whose members sincerely believe in the moral goodness that justifies the schools' existence, have a common understanding of what they want to accomplish, and share ideas about how they can reach their goals. To develop such schools, we need to understand several important overlapping and interconnected concepts, seven of which we discuss here:

- Culture, particularly culture as it applies to organizations
- Community
- Unity of purpose
- Learning as the central purpose of schools
- Teachers as professional experts and primary decision makers for schools
- An authentic atmosphere for learning
- Optimism

Schools as Cultures

Anthropologists use the concept of *culture* to provide meaning for how people behave. Culture is typically defined as a pattern of behavior, assumptions, and beliefs that sets a group apart from others. It includes subconcepts, such as identity, values, beliefs, rituals, traditions, norms, leaders, leadership, and loyalty. It encompasses characteristics that hold a group together—values that a people share, common ways of thinking and behaving, a sense of history, and a body of accepted traditions. Those within a group identify with the group's culture, and that identity creates a feeling of belonging. It enables people to fit in, to know how to act, and to predict how others will act. It provides a sense of security for individuals that says they are not alone, that others care about them, and that they share a common purpose (Myers & Myers, 1995, pp. 120-126).

That schools embody the characteristics of culture is obvious to anyone who enters a school building. It can be seen in the patterns of school organization, interpersonal relationships, personal loyalties, the roles various individuals play, folklore, rituals, symbols—and most of all in the commitment to a mission (see Bolman & Deal, 1991; Deal & Kennedy, 1982).

The moral mission of schools to educate students not only justifies their existence, it also sustains them over time and provides direction for all they do. That moral mission provides a glue that holds the people and all the other elements of a school together, inspires hard work, bridges times of frustration, and reinforces commitment and dedication to students and society. It not only sets schools apart from all other institutions, including all other places where people work, but it also places teachers in a professional context different from all other workers (Barth, 1990; Fullan, 1993; Sergiovanni, 1992, 1996).

A number of scholars have described organizations of many types as cultures and they have noted the similarities between school cultures and the cultures of other organizations, especially businesses and corporations; many have recommended that schools adopt a number of the ideas of corporate organizational cultures as they attempt to make themselves better. For example, Terrence Deal and Allen Kennedy (1982) explain the life, operation, and leadership roles in corporations in cultural terms and advise corporate leaders to use cultural ideas—such as purposely constructed norms, rituals, celebrations, symbols, and traditions—to create worker identity, loyalty, and motivation. They suggest that the same ideas can, and should, be applied by school leaders to their organizations and to the school workers over whom they have leadership responsibility.

Scholars such as Deal and Kennedy (1982) have provided a great service to school leaders by directing their attention to the concept of culture as a primary metaphor for schools and to anthropology and sociology as guiding disciplines. Their thinking has provided more useful tools for understanding and improving schools than the ideas of the past. Educators now look for the values and feelings that draw teachers and students together for the hard work of schooling; they can identify cultural aspects of the school lives of all participants that can be improved on so that those lives can be made more positive and more meaningful and they can rely on intrinsic motivators for good work instead of artificially contrived ones. In fact, the idea of culture as it has been applied to organizations has played a large part in school reform efforts since the 1980s; it has guided a number of good school improvement projects, such as the Coalition of Essential Schools (Muncey & McQuillan, 1996).

Schools as Anthropologists See Them

Despite the value of this thinking, however, the concept of organizational culture as developed in business and then applied to schools falls short of fully explaining the culture of schools, and a shift in thinking is now in order, one that takes schools beyond most corporate culture thinking. This shift in thinking is necessary not because schools are not cultures but because schools are not businesses.

Probably because the thinking of the corporate culture writers broke new ground, many cultural insights now being applied to schools have not come directly from anthropology but have come indirectly, by way of the corporate world (Deal & Kennedy, 1982; Peters & Waterman, 1982). That initial application of cultural insights to business required some tinkering with, and narrowing of, the original anthropological concepts to make them fit that setting. As those slightly transformed ideas have been shifted from business to schools, they have carried with them the business-oriented modifications they picked up along the way. School leaders now need to look to the original anthropological versions of the concept of culture, along with all its subconcepts, instead of to the versions that have evolved for businesses and other corporate purposes.

Business leaders have tended to "manufacture" cultural ideas in their organizations; in doing so, they have used an approach to organizational improvement that does not fit schools. As business leaders apply cultural ideas to their organizations, they quickly see the value of traditions, rituals, and symbols as devices to bring cohesion among and motivate their workers. So they turn to traditions and symbols that have been lying dormant in their company's past and to new ones that they construct to fit specific motivational needs. They dredge up or manufacture mission statements, stories of past accomplishments, printed symbols, and logos—and impress them on their workers as extrinsic motivators. As Deal and Kennedy point out, Mary Kay Cosmetics has its bumblebee, the U.S. Marines has its "few good men," and Saturn has its emergency button that any worker can use to stop the entire assembly line if he or she judges that it is important to do so (see Deal & Kennedy, 1982; Deal & Peterson, 1994).

Frequently, school leaders who learn about corporate cultural techniques are impressed and quickly try to create their own. They write mission statements and post them in school lobbies, they display easy-to-remember motivational sayings on bulletin boards and school letterhead, and they unfurl banners proclaiming "School of Excellence." Their thinking runs somewhat like this: These cultural devices seem to work in business organizations; this is an organization similar to businesses, so these devices should work here.

When school leaders adopt their cultural devices from business in this way, they usually create artificial symbols and motivators even though more effective motivators are already inherent in the school culture and present in the very acts of learning and teaching. The best culturally based motivators are available for students in the act of learning itself and for teachers in the form of (1) a noticeably well-taught group of students, (2) recognized student successes, and (3) the sincere thanks expressed by students, graduating students, and former students who return to school years later (see Lortie, 1975). Instead of following the corporate world by manufacturing motivators, school leaders need only to highlight the moral purposes of schools and give those who do the good work of learning and teaching better recognition.

Noticeably better schools are more likely to come about because sincere, competent students and teachers work together to accomplish the school's clear moral purpose—learning—than because of leader-devised, artificial, extrinsic rewards. School communities should work hard at clarifying their learning mission and genuinely explore its implications for all students and society; they do not need to manufacture any other reasons to justify why they exist and what they do.

Schools as Communities

Thinking of schools as *communities* as well as cultures distinguishes them even more from most other organizations and helps us understand them from an additional perspective. It enables us to see them as something like extended families, tribal clans, or cohesive neighborhoods. Unlike most businesses, internal community affiliations are intended to draw participants together rather than produce a product, and interpersonal associations involve stronger attachments and deeper commitments. Their bonds transcend those necessary to get the work done and to justify being paid.

In contrast, business organizations exist to produce a product or provide services. They have cultures, of course, and those cultures may enable the organizations to accomplish their purposes, as is the case with the Total Quality Management movement, which focuses heavily on customer service as a basis for all management decisions (Bonstingl, 1992; Murgatroyd & Morgan, 1993). Business leaders who subscribe to the total quality management philosophy strive to make quality customer service the core element in their way of doing things. So cultural aspects of business organizations are attended to and emphasized for this purpose: Corporate histories are resurrected and celebrated, heroes are recognized more often and more noticeably, and logos and slogans are created and displayed more prominently— not because of an inherent sense of community among people, but because corporate leaders have orchestrated a culturally based positive feeling among employees, one that results in better and more profitably produced products and services.

Extended family cultures, on the other hand, have different beginning points, different ties, and different emphases. Although we can say they exist to "produce" a successful next generation of family members, to think of families in such narrow terms is misleading, if not insulting. Families, at least good ones, are much more than reproductive agencies, and their extra elements are what distinguishes a "good" family from a not-so-good one. Family members care about each other, help each other, rely on each other, protect each other, have emotional attachments to each other, and take pride in each other. Their reasons for being are many, the interpersonal connections are numerous and often hard to detect, and a sense of belonging rather than accomplishment holds the family together. Being a family, or being a member of a family, is more important than any set of goals that a family could establish and accomplish.

Although school communities may not fit exactly the mold of extended families, clans, or tightly knit neighborhoods, they can be conceived of as more like extended families than like corporations. Although schools are not families, they are more of a community as seen by anthropologists than organizational communities in a corporate context.

When schools are looked on as communities in this way, a number of cultural characteristics become visible. Relationships and ideas among people hold them together. Distinctiveness is appropriate, necessary, and encouraged. People belong because of who they are rather than what role they play. Roles and responsibilities of individuals get mixed up and shift without people realizing it. Values, caring, and people-to-people attachments are more important than rules, regulations, or enforced right ways of doing things. Persuasion is more important than regulation. Leaders act more like heads of clans and tribal chiefs than like managers and engineers (Deal & Kennedy, 1982; Sergiovanni, 1992, 1996).

Unity of Purpose

When the singular nature of the moral purpose or mission of schools—to create learning—is agreed to whole-heartedly by all community members, that mission can provide the glue that holds school communities together. It can provide a foundation on which shared values and beliefs can develop, a sense of interpersonal connectedness can evolve, and personal bonds can form. That mission—and the shared values, loyalties, and bonds that grow from it—can then set the norms that guide behavior, give meaning to day-to-day activities, and establish group and personal direction.

When school community members possess this *unity of purpose,* they know what their school is about. They know where they, as a group, are going. They work toward agreement on priorities. They have compatible images of each other. They know each other's strengths, weaknesses, and predilections. They help each other toward their common goals. They value and like what they do. They are proud of their community's uniqueness and accomplishments. They share its struggles and failures. They work toward making their school community fit comfortably into the larger school system community and into the student, parent, and neighborhood communities that their school serves and of which it is a part. They can temper their subgroup goals, loyalties, and norms for the good of the school community as a whole, and, more important, they realize how necessary it is to do so (Barth, 1990; Lambert et al., 1995, 1997; Noddings, 1992).

More Than Delivering Services

One educational authority who sees schools as purpose-based communities, Thomas Sergiovanni (1992), contrasts the type of school community we are talking about with the idea of school as a delivery system, and he suggests that schools that are thought of as delivery systems rather than purpose-based communities probably revolve around the following themes:

- How to identify and carefully develop the targets, goals, steps, procedures, timetables, and schedules that will become the basis for establishing the best routes for delivering instruction
- How to train deliverers properly and then provide them with clear instructions for what to do
- How to develop a system of monitoring to ensure that instruction is delivered properly
- How to provide additional training to correct mistakes and align what deliverers do with what they are supposed to do
- How to establish an evaluation scheme that measures the extent to which the system is working (pp. 45-46)

In comparison, he suggests that schools that function as purpose-based communities are more concerned with the following:

- How the learning community is defined
- What the relationships are among parents, students, teachers, and administrators
- What shared values, purposes, and commitments bond the community
- How parents, teachers, administrators, and students work together to embody these values
- What kinds of obligations members have to the community and how these are enforced (p. 46)

The unity of purpose aspect of a school community's mission, when it is cultivated successfully, creates an emotional-level attachment to that community. It instills a sense of mission similar to what some people would describe as a "calling," and that calling stimulates a unifying, heartfelt commitment by all community members to pursue the mission. The mission is the reason why the school exists and the basis on which it justifies what it does. It is both the compass that sets direction and the motivator that prompts action. All school community participants—teachers, administrators, staff members, students, and parents—understand and accept the mission as that which gives their individual roles and work legitimacy (Glickman, 1993).

But a sense of mission is more than a superficial understanding and acceptance of mission. It includes a commitment that is deeper and more personally involving. It is akin to what Sergiovanni (1992) refers to as a school's *covenant,* a "binding and solemn agreement . . . that represents a value system for living together and forms the basis of decisions and actions" (p. 73).

This unifying purpose of a school community cannot be imposed on people because artificial efforts to build community and mission are counterproductive. Instead, it grows from what community members value, the ideas to which they subscribe, and the work that they do, not from what they produce or ideas developed by their leaders (Barth, 1990; Hargreaves & Dawe, 1990). Although some well-recognized writers in the field of school leadership think of a school's mission as a core of ideas developed by school leaders and transmitted by those leaders to teacher-followers, we prefer to think that the mission rests in ideas and values intrinsic to the community as a whole. All participants, including administrators, recognize, accept, and are guided by these ideas and values. No one is superior to them. In learning community schools, good school leaders articulate, reflect, clarify, and cultivate a mission that exists apart from them in the community at large.

Learning as the Central Purpose of Schools

Thus far in our discussion of schools as morally based learning communities, we have described their cultural and community characteristics, the importance of their moral mission, and the significance of the fact that that mission is focused on a single purpose—the best possible learning for all students. We now look more directly at the significance of learning as the school community's central purpose and mission (also see Barth, 1990).

School communities that see student learning as their true mission and singular purpose operate from a position of moral authority—they understand that creating learning is morally good work. That moral base guides their decisions, demands their difficult work, fosters their professional relationships, sustains them through hard times, and keeps group goals on a priority level above individual ones. Because learning is virtuous, community members are motivated by inner urges, personally formed obligations and commitments, and professional norms for doing their work well. The moral base, with its shared values and beliefs, provides guidance as well as affirms decisions made. Every decision does not have to be the correct one and every consequence does not have to be the best of all those possible as long as the mission and efforts to achieve it are virtuous. Of course, decisions cannot be made carelessly or irresponsibly and consequences cannot be disregarded, but well-thought-through experimentation intended to help students learn is more valued than "playing it safe" when student learning can be improved.

Unfortunately, many school leaders today often make decisions because of other factors: for example, they try to cut costs, look good for influential sectors of the public, please higher-level administrators, avoid hassles, or accommodate bus and lunch schedules. Also, any number of intrusive conditions can arise in the normal lives of schools that may divert energies: For example, school administrators typically assign too many students with broad ranges of abilities to a single class and teacher and without providing adequate support. They usually rationalize such actions with statements about how capable the teacher is and how well he or she can handle difficult-to-manage students, when in fact they are basing their decision on cost factors, administrative convenience, and efforts to avoid hassles. In our view, any time a school decision is made on any basis other than an honest desire for the best learning for all students, the school is not being guided by student learning as its mission.

Of course, no schools and no individuals within school communities are perfect, and school decisions are made and activities pursued for many different reasons. As long as these reasons fit compatibly and justifiably with the moral purpose of student learning, and as long as they contribute honestly to that overall purpose, at least in the long run, we probably have no serious reason for concern. When decisions and actions are made without vigilant and serious attention to how they affect student learning, however, we have reason to complain. When this happens as a normal way of operating a school, the school has lost its compass.

In learning community schools, the moral purpose of student learning guides not only school-level decisions but decisions at all levels, including those made by individual teachers in their classrooms, by school district administrators, and by teacher educators who prepare and provide continuing instruction for teacher practitioners. When teachers are deciding what to test for in third-grade mathematics, when policy makers are deciding what to fund at what levels, and when college educators are deciding what to teach future teachers about constructivist approaches to learning, all are guided by the same moral-based question, What is best for pre-K-12 student learning?

What does this mean in practical terms? How can teachers, teacher leaders, and teacher educators in learning community schools act differently from the way most now do? In short, they can and do ask more questions. First, they ask of themselves, their colleagues, their administrators, and their teacher educators, Will what we are considering or what we are about to do help or hinder student learning? In what ways? For which students? If some students will not benefit immediately, what greater good in terms of student learning will be served? Is the trade-off worth it? Second, in considering these questions, they consistently distinguish means for accomplishing goals and the overall mission itself. For example, they might agree to organize the school day around the bus and lunch schedules because doing so serves as means for securing a smooth school day and attracts the cooperation of administrators and school support staff. This, in turn, is likely to promote better teaching and learning. But they will not confuse the means with the mission of student learning because at some point a bus schedule or the pleasure of administrators might become so contradictory to student learning that it could not be agreed to.

Teachers as Professional Experts and Primary Decision Makers

Because student learning is the central mission of the school culture and community, teaching is seen as the paramount professional task; therefore, community norms consider teachers to be the predominant experts and decision makers for the entire school community enterprise. Everyone in the community knows that teachers are the professionals on the scene and closest to the learning of students. Teachers know individual students better than anyone else, and they understand students' learning strengths and weaknesses, how they interact with each other as a class, what and how much they have already learned, and much more.

Because teachers are recognized as the experts on the scene, what they decide and what they do guides all school community activities. Other decisions emanate from and revolve around them. Although teachers are expected to follow established rules, guidelines, and norms, they know that schools cannot be run by prescription and learning cannot be created by remote control—that is, from outside the classroom. Instead, teachers themselves apply the laws, rules, and policies based on what their professional judgment tells them is best for their students (Bolman & Deal, 1991; Fullan, 1992a; Glickman, 1993; Lambert et al., 1995, 1997; Weiss, 1993, 1995).

A Whole School Responsibility

Because the community places this professional responsibility with teachers, teachers must be committed to education in a very broad sense—to the education of not only the students assigned to them but to the entire school community. Poor teaching down the hall, a colleague in need of professional assistance, equipment that is broken, and materials that do not arrive on time are not someone else's problem; they are everyone's responsibility. In learning community schools, teachers, as a group of colleagues, create learning experiences for all students, and they are powerful enough to secure the conditions and resources necessary to do so. Moreover, they believe that they can succeed, that it is both possible and realistic for their school community to accomplish its moral mission.

Because teachers are seen as the professional experts in charge of all learning of the entire learning community school, the community also considers teachers to be responsible for their own professional development. They design and carry out plans for their own improvement—realizing along the way that learning to teach better requires much more than implementing the messages of others—from show-and-tell workshops, supervisors, consultants, or an instructor's manual. As a result, learning to teach better becomes a normal part of what respected teachers do automatically. The norms expect that those who are not competent enough to perform knowledgeably and skillfully will become competent and, as professionals, they are responsible for their own competence as well as that of their colleagues. Those norms also expect that teachers who are incapable of being developed to an acceptable level of competence must be replaced, and professional colleagues must see that this happens (see Sergiovanni, 1996).

A Different Attitude About Expertise

These norms of teachers as professional experts and primary decision makers of schools are not consistent with the technical-managerial ways in which many schools now operate. Most schools of today assume a top-down flow of responsibilities and a bottom-up flow of accountabilities and place teachers and students at the bottom. They assume that people in upper-level administrative and supervisory positions know better than teachers what and how they should be teaching. They assume teachers are routine-level workers who should be told prescriptively what to do and then watched closely to make sure they have followed directions. This attitude has embedded in it the belief that poor teaching results from teachers either not knowing what to do or not being motivated enough to do the good work they are capable of doing. So the manager or supervisor shows teachers what to do and uses rewards, incentives, and punishments to force them to do it.

This type of thinking is not consistent with a learning community professional atmosphere in which teachers exercise the authority and responsibility that they should exercise as professional investigative experts. In learning community settings, professional decisions that affect students are not handed down in a bureaucratic chain of command. They are made by professionals who know, believe in, and are part of the local learning community. They are made by those who carry them to their conclusion and who have a personal stake in their success. They are made by those close enough to their implementation so that adjustments can be made along the way. And they are made by professionals who have the freedom, support, and resources necessary to do the job expected of them.

Form Follows Function

When teachers lead school communities in this way, they base their decisions on two major considerations: (1) what they want their students to learn, and (2) how they can best stimulate it. For competent, caring teachers, the decision-making process follows a rather simple path; one that can be summed up in the expression *form follows function.* The *functions* of quality teaching and creating learning experiences for students provide the bases for teacher decisions and the forms that develop around schools—such as specific curriculum arrangements, patterns of school organization, class schedules, the shape and configurations of buildings, and teacher in-service education programs—all flow from these functions (see Block, 1993).

This flow runs counter to basic assumptions of some current reform, restructuring, and partnership endeavors—those that not only ignore the importance of teachers' investigative expertise and commitment but see the apparent unwillingness of teachers to change as the primary stumbling block to improving schools. These efforts at restructuring concentrate on changing *forms* in the hope of forcing teachers to change what they do. Frequent examples of this are when administrators impose block scheduling, multigrade teaching, "back-to-basics" curricula, or cross-disciplinary instruction on teachers. In these cases, the administrators seem to blame teachers because some students do not learn as well as they should, and they impose changes in the teachers' working arrangements to force them to modify their ways of teaching. In essence, they modify the circumstances under which teachers teach and demand that teachers conform to the modified circumstances. They push for change in schools without engaging the leadership, knowledge, and collaborative support of teachers and the profession.

This top-to-bottom or outside-in approach to reform is unnecessary. As we have seen, a more effective approach is to involve teachers—to allow them to accept responsibility for how their school is now and for what it can become, have them decide what needs to be modified so they can teach better, then do what they say and collegially assess the consequences. Teaching can then be better because it starts with teachers—the key change agents—and builds on their commitments, goals, and ideas; it accepts and reinforces teacher responsibility. If the process is done well, at least three positive outcomes are likely: (1) teachers assume responsibility for changes and the results of those changes at the school level, (2) better informed decisions are made, and (3) change becomes a continuing, self-sustaining part of teachers' professional lives.

Blaming teachers' stubbornness for their resistance to change reflects a short-sighted, superficial understanding of change, the professional roles and responsibilities of teachers, and school environments. It ignores possible reasons behind teacher reluctance and assumes that teachers neither believe in their mission nor are guided by what is best for their students. Although this is a valid criticism of some teachers, it is not for most. When teachers resist change, we should interpret this not as a cause of school problems but as a symptom of other problems. We can then investigate deeper reasons for the resistance. Some teachers may oppose changes that they perceive as being harmful to students; if they believe this, they have a moral obligation to oppose the changes. Good teachers in learning community schools would do no less—inaction would be irresponsible.

An Authentic Atmosphere for Learning

As the professional experts and primary decision makers in learning community schools, teachers are also responsible for creating and maintaining an *authentic atmosphere for learning*—primarily with their teacher colleagues but also among all community participants. Ideally, in such an atmosphere everyone accepts learning as an agreed-on high priority and engages in it seriously and honestly—listening to each other, thinking, reflecting, pondering, and explaining—without posturing, competing for recognition as an intellectual superior, or looking down at others. Everyone studies and inquires together as a community of thinkers and, as a result, both the community and individual members grow. Participants openly exchange ideas and perspectives and try to understand each other's thinking. In team-like fashion, they pursue a progressive, communitywide compatibility of thought that, at times, might approach like-mindedness (Barth, 1990; Lambert et al., 1995, 1997).

Cultivating such an atmosphere is, of course, a difficult and never-ending task because individual teachers, like all people, understand and see things differently and base their thinking on different values and beliefs. They are diverse and they often find it hard to reign in their personal ideas and assumptions enough to learn from others. The challenges of the task are, therefore, to develop a shared identity, common commitments to mutual goals, and a compatibility of day-to-day practices, and to do so among diversity and individuality.

Long ago, John Dewey (1916/1944) suggested that the kind of atmosphere we are discussing here could be developed if communities cultivate among their members three key elements that could draw everyone together and nurture interpersonal associations once they begin to evolve. He identifies the elements as *communication, commonalities,* and *democracy,* and he has rather particular ideas for each. We explain our interpretations of these ideas next and describe how they interact to forge an authentic learning community.

Communication

Communication is the open, unencumbered, intellectual interaction among community participants. Its purposes are to pursue the community mission and goals, to share ideas and perspectives as a means for doing so, and to enlighten all who participate. It expands everyone's knowledge, deepens their understanding, develops their competencies, cultivates their values, and stimulates their desire to probe and grow.

Commonalities

Commonalities are sets of beliefs, purposes, goals, experiences, and understandings communicated to and accepted by community members as they interact. They are things such as common religious dogmas that hold church members together, common work experiences for employees, and holiday dinners for extended families. They are the bases for freely and genuinely accepted like-mindedness. For teachers, commonalities might include school rules, norms, having lunch together, athletic events, and traditions of all kinds.

Democracy

When many of us think of democracy, we are inclined to think of the idea in its political context, as a form of government, a set of values that protect people in some fashion, or laws and principles that allow people to vote in elections. But here we use democracy differently. We use it to mean an openness and equality among community participants. When seen in this way, democracy is primarily a way of living in communities in which people freely communicate their own experiences and thoughts with one another so they can learn from one another, rather than push on others their own personal previously held views. In this idea of democracy, when two people communicate, both learn—the communicator and the listener both share experiences that broaden their understanding. When it is present in classrooms, students and teachers, no matter how diverse their backgrounds, help each other grow educationally.

Michael Apple and James Beane (1995) suggest that the democracy that we are talking about entails at least the following:

- The open flow of ideas, regardless of their popularity, that enables people to be as fully informed as possible
- Faith in the individual and collective capacity of people to create possibilities for resolving problems
- The use of critical reflection and analysis to evaluate ideas, problems, and policies
- Concern for the welfare of others and the common good
- Concern for the dignity and rights of individuals and minorities
- An understanding that democracy is not so much an "ideal" to be pursued as an "idealized" set of values that we must live and that must guide our life as a people
- The organization of social institutions to promote and extend the democratic way of life

The Interaction of Communication, Commonalities, and Democracy

The authentic atmosphere for learning that is so necessary for learning community schools develops through an evolving communication about commonalities and differences in intellectually democratic settings. Ideally, community participants share ideas with each other and, in doing so, find out what one another think. As they listen and reflect, they identify more and more commonalities that build community and serve as the basis for more communication. The sequence continues as long as the communication is open and honest—as long as it is educative for all.

More specifically, teachers communicate their ideas to one another formally and informally and, as they do, they come to understand the perspectives of others—their colleagues and other community participants and stakeholders. When the communication occurs among these individuals on a regular basis, the reasons the various people hold certain ideas and beliefs or the absence of such reasons become more apparent. A common understanding of what others really think emerges as an important commonality of the community. Differences of opinion as well as agreed-on values and common understandings and needs become visible. This visibility of values and beliefs permits even greater understanding and appreciation of one another. Discussions of differences also lead to greater understanding and, sometimes, to an appreciation of diversity and to the changing of minds about differences and common interests and concerns.

Over time, people living in the community continue to communicate with one another; they develop a set of common emotional and intellectual attachments. One of these attachments, according to Dewey (1916/1944), is a common concern on the part of everyone in the community for the reasons, arguments, evidence, perspectives, opinions, and beliefs expressed by all other members.

Although regular communication is essential to guarantee community, however, it is not sufficient. The communication may occur in only an honorific, not genuine, sense and may divide people rather than bring them together around common values and practices. If the communication is not genuinely valued, nothing much is imparted, shared, discovered, conveyed, made known, revealed, created, passed on, received, constructed, or opened up—nothing much is learned. On the other hand, if communication is valued, it can enhance the development of other important commonalities and help educate the community. So intellectually democratic communication has a high priority in learning communities.

In this context, the evolving commonalities provide a theoretical lattice either for keeping educational priorities and practices in place and unchanged or for initiating educational change or renewal. They frame the purpose of educating students in morally defensible and educationally productive ways; because of this, they are important to a community that is expecting to become better. They provide a unity that energizes change.

Diversity as a Commonality

It is important to acknowledge that the growth of commonalities occurs in pluralistic and diverse cultures as well as in homogeneous ones as long as the community is intellectually democratic. In fact, a school or society characterized by diversity provides an opportunity for everyone of different cultures, races, religions, and economic groups both to escape the confining elements of his or her own traditions and environment and to help others grow and escape the limiting features of their settings. In short, intermingling ideas and understandings in democratic environments with others of diverse backgrounds is educatively valuable to everyone involved (Dewey, 1916/1944, pp. 20-21).

When diversity is looked at in this way, it can be a valued commonality, an asset. Differences become valued, in part, because they are means for expanding understanding and escaping the limiting features of one's own culture. For teachers and other occupational groups, the expanded understanding that emerges from formal and informal interaction among all community members constitutes a commonality, a vehicle to other commonalities, and an agency to reach beyond personal, cultural, and educational boundaries. Every teacher's prior experiences are in some ways both limiting and liberating, confining and emancipating; therefore, when teachers interact and communicate with one another and their students, they, with their students, can grow beyond their prior experiences and learn to share a more common cultural and pedagogical ground. This concept of educative diversity can be seen when teachers who tend to follow unquestioningly the lead of principals, informal school leaders, and college professors are joined by new faculty members who readily challenge authority and assert their own beliefs. Soon, some of the "more liberated" ideas rub off on the more cautious colleagues.

When learning communities develop in ideal form, what Dewey (1916/1944) calls a "common mind," a "common intent," and a "common understanding" emerge and these commonalities help make the community what it is. But how a common mind, intent, and understanding evolve must be watched carefully. They cannot be forced on anyone. If some individuals think and act differently, they should not be compelled to change their minds or behaviors and they should not be forced or manipulated into accepting the understandings and behaviors that most community members embrace. Communities are not enhanced by conformity, so community members should not demand uniformity of values, thought, or practice of their colleagues.

To the extent that a group of teachers has a set of common understandings and values that look toward what their school community can become and to the extent that the group consciously works to achieve goals that emerge from these understandings and values, they constitute the kind of learning community we envision. When these same understandings and values are a part of teacher and student cultures, they stimulate growth and direction and help enable a school to become an even stronger learning community. In the absence of a set of common beliefs and values to motivate activities, there appears to be little reason to think of a group of teachers as a community and a school as a community of learners—there is little reason to believe that schooling will be focused and educative or that educational change and renewal of any significance will occur.

When taken together, communication, commonalities, and democracy help form intellectually open communities—communities in which commonalities develop from free inquiry and in which ideas and values are personally constructed through individual and group investigation. In such communities, although something similar to unanimity of thought might develop sometimes, unanimity is neither sought for its own sake nor forced. The agreement and consensus that develop evolve through honest study and learning by all community participants. This is the essence of inquiry in the learning communities that we envision.

A Sense of Optimism

Even when schools function as learning communities, they are not likely to achieve their goals unless community members believe that those goals are achievable. Underlying that belief must be a sense of optimism, one based on knowing that the community possesses the knowledge, competence, resources, support, and organizational environment necessary to succeed in educating students. Optimism is important because reaching a significant goal requires persistent effort over time, and most efforts confront periods of frustration. Optimism based on pedagogical realities provides the sustaining power, the will to persevere. It supplies the resilience that all professionals need from time to time.

When professional knowledge and competence or school resources are inadequate, the task of getting better becomes more difficult than it should be and the sustaining power of a positive outlook fades over time. On the other hand, no school setting has unlimited knowledge, competence, and resources, so to be successful, school

communities need a balance between realistic goals and the resources needed to achieve them. Optimism preserves the balance.

Successful school communities develop, cultivate, and maintain
an optimistic attitude that sustains all their members and underlies all
their efforts—especially student learning. Every community member
believes that all members can learn in significant ways and that they
will continue to learn in important respects because of their participation in the community.

Optimistic school community members see learning as continuous, building over time to higher levels, successively reinforcing, and
exciting. They confidently anticipate the learning that is yet to come.
Their optimism is not unfounded or naive, but is strong and pervasive
enough to motivate, to bridge times of difficulty, to carry along those
who have doubts, and to sustain the belief in each community member's mind that he or she has a hand in shaping and advancing the
good work of the school.

In commenting about optimism in terms of American society as a
whole, John W. Gardner (1981) says the following:

> The capacity of our people to believe stubbornly and irrepressibly
> that this is a world worth saving, and that intelligence and energy
> and good will might save it, is one of the most endearing and brac-
> ing of American traits. . . . If we lose that optimism we will surely
> be a less spirited people, a less magnanimous people and an im-
> measurably less venturesome people. Zest and generosity will dis-
> appear from our national style. And our impact on the world may
> well disappear along with them. (p. 114)

The same idea applies to school communities and their members.

Learning as Experience-Based Intellectual Construction

Learning that occurs in learning community schools is (1) personal intellectual construction that occurs while learners engage in
school experiences, rather than the transmission of ideas, skills, and
values from teachers to learners; (2) something that happens in individuals, instead of something that happens to them; and (3) something
that happens while the experience is occurring rather than as a result
of it. It is measured by how learners change rather than by what they

gain or achieve (Barth, 1990; Brooks & Gernnon-Brooks, 1993; Eisner, 1991, 1992, 1993; Lambert et al., 1995, 1997; Sergiovanni, 1992, 1994, 1996). This idea of learning is much like that experienced by John Holt (see Chapter 1; Canfield & Hansen, 1993) in learning to play the cello and playing the cello.

The idea of learning as possessing these characteristics is quite different from the way learning is typically thought of today; the difference is more than semantic. It has implications for defining what happens in schools, what students and teachers do, why they do what they do, and how students, teachers, schools, and teacher educators are assessed. It means that educators assess their work by how well they provide the experience of learning rather than by measuring what has been learned. This, in turn, means that learning is truly the central moral purpose of schools and teaching. As a result of this thinking, a number of other very good things happen. Students (and their teachers) pursue learning for its own sake rather than to get a good grade, to avoid failing a test, or to have a good class average. They begin to see that it is okay for learners to be in the process of learning rather than having already learned whatever is under study. For example, they can be learning mathematics even if they cannot solve every problem correctly. They can admit that they do not know something as yet, are not yet able to do something with proficiency, and are still sorting out their values. They are less likely to fear failure or public embarrassment for not having achieved, and are less likely to worry about meeting teachers', classmates', and parents' expectations. Instead, the desire, challenge, and fun of learning become the learners' self-motivators, sustainers of hard work, and personal rewards. Challenge and inquisitiveness become as important as externally assigned grades. Optimism replaces anxiety. The dominant teacher-student relationship becomes more like that of coach and trainee than of reward manipulator and manipulated performer.

Learning as Contrasted With Achieving

In learning community schools, assessment, achievement, and rewards for success are important, but they have to do with measuring learning, are not in themselves learning, and are not the best reasons for learning. They tell where a learner is on a specific scale at a specific time, but they do not certify that a learner has completed learning—because learning is never complete.

When learners experience something, anything, they are changed in some way by that experience and that change is, in fact, learning. Students learn even when they do not learn what is on the test—or when they learn some of the tested material but still receive a failing grade, fall below the class average, or do not meet their teachers' expectations. They learn even if they have not learned "enough" in someone's estimation (and "learning enough" has more to do with the meaning of enough than it has to do with learning).

Many people confuse assessment and achievement with learning at least partly because they think of schools as factories and delivery systems. Factories exist to produce products, and delivery systems exist to bring something from somewhere else to those who should receive it. When we think of schools in these ways, it is only logical to look for products—to look for what students receive from teachers. Results and the receiving of something are what matter, and their presence or absence is used to assess whether or not students, teachers, and schools are good enough. So we look for results and for what students get from their teachers and their classes—for what they achieve. We test for results and we ask, Are these results as good as we expected? How do they compare with the results of other schools, classes, teachers, and students?

When we think of learning in this different way—as a process—tests provide a different and more appropriate function. They are a means for checking individual student progress, for guiding future teaching, and for deciding what to do next; and they are devices for pushing everyone—students and teachers (and presumably parents)—toward more and harder work. They are used more to guide and motivate students and teachers and to redistribute school resources and personnel than to serve as evidence of what has been accomplished.

The concept of learning as experienced-based intellectual construction is critical to the functioning of learning community schools because it defines both why such schools exist and what they do. To illustrate, we now describe in more detail four key elements of this conceptualization of learning that we have already touched on briefly:

- Learning as experience
- Learning as intellectual construction
- Learning in the school community as a whole
- The learning of teachers

Learning as Experience

When we think of learning as experience—experience similar to performing in an orchestra or playing on an athletic team, rather than producing measured achievement results—our priorities change. Although the classroom equivalent of the sound of the applause or the final numbers on the scoreboard is not inconsequential, it is not the reason for participating. It does not show all that has been learned and it does not signal that learning has ended. Learners participate in learning events for the experience. The experience embodies the learning; the test results, the score, and the praise reflect only someone else's measure of it at a particular time.

With this change in thinking, we can visualize a parallel between learning and gardening. When gardening is engaged in because of the satisfaction derived from the experience, it is similar to our idea of learning as experience. As gardeners-for-the-satisfaction-of-it engage in the activities of gardening, they increase their knowledge and develop expertise, and these gains enhance their enjoyment and satisfaction. They learn and get better at gardening at the same time. Although they produce beautiful flowers and might even sell some, their primary purposes are participating in the activity of gardening and becoming better gardeners. Commercial gardeners, on the other hand, have different purposes and motives. Their gardening is for profit, and they assess their activity in terms of results. For them, gardening is work. They do it for the money instead of the experience. (See Sergiovanni, 1996, pp. 27-32, for a gardening analogy about the aesthetic qualities of school communities.)

This idea of learning as being developed in experience has at least four direct implications for teaching and teachers. First, it helps us see teachers not as producers of products—learned students or learning in students—but as creators of experiences. Second, we can begin to see assessment, including tests, not as reports about products but as monitoring devices. Third, we can look at teacher-student relationships not as those of providers and receivers of information, skills, and values but as coaches and trainees. Fourth, we can see teaching as learning—as a process of intellectual construction for teachers as well as students, one in which they continue to learn to teach at the same time that they are teaching.

When teaching is seen as this process of intellectual construction, teachers do not always have to know everything about an idea, be proficient in a skill, or have clearly formulated values before they present them to students. They can be seen as continuous and developing learners who learn from their day-to-day teaching, from their classes and individual students, and from reflecting on their practice. They do not have to be seen as fully defined experts who have already learned all they need to learn and are simply applying their previously learned knowledge, skills, and value perspectives to a new group of students in a setting only slightly different from last year. When teachers are seen in this way, they can serve as examples of lifelong learners for their students.

Seeing learning in this way also has important implications for school principals and other administrators—both in how they relate to teachers and how they learn. First, it shifts their relationships with teachers toward the role of teacher educator rather than manager of teacher behavior. They begin to help, coach, and provide services much more as they assist teacher experts improve their teaching and their students' learning. As with the changed relationship between teachers and students that we already mentioned, this means that principals and other administrators do not have to know everything about good teaching. Helping teachers need not mean telling, showing, directing, manipulating, and forcing. It can, and should, mean providing encouragement, ideas, information, time, and resources; providing for teacher colleagues mutually beneficial learning experiences; and removing obstacles so teachers can learn as they teach and, therefore, teach as best as they can and get better in the process (Barth 1988, 1990).

Second, it means that administrators also learn on the job. Just as teachers learn from teaching, students learn from learning, cello players learn from playing the cello, and gardeners learn from gardening, administrators learn from administering. If they conceive of their work appropriately, they are always learning and becoming better leaders—and learners—in the process.

Learning as Intellectual Construction

In learning community schools, learners develop what they know by fitting new ideas together with ideas they have already learned from previous experience, and they do this fitting together in their own unique ways. In the process of making these intellectual constructions, they are influenced by the social and intellectual environments in which they find themselves. As a result, because much learning occurs in schools and classrooms, these settings affect both how and what learners learn.

This constructivist learning process is often explained by using Jean Piaget's (1950) concepts of adaptation, assimilation, and accommodation. When this explanation is provided in a school context, it can be described as follows: Learners see or hear something in their school environment (or experience it in some other way), interpret that new experience based on what they already know, and come to a personal understanding by connecting the new experience with their previous understanding. The result of the process is learning that is made up of three elements: (1) knowledge they gain from the new experience, (2) their prior understanding, and (3) their personal connection of the new and the old. Because the learner's previous understanding is unique and because the intellectual process he or she uses to make the connection is unique as well, the construction is personally unique to each individual (see Lambert et al., 1995, 1997; Lord, 1994; Wheatley, 1991; Yager, 1993).

Suppose, for example, a teacher reads aloud a story of a fire burning out of control and consuming a building. Suppose that one of the children in the class has experienced a similar fire in the past and was seriously burned. The other children have had no such experience. Upon hearing about the fire, the one child becomes emotionally upset and fearful; the others are intrigued but neither upset nor fearful. Why? Individual children construct different meanings about the fire in the story based on their understanding and experience and their interpretation of what they hear.

Learning that is constructed occurs continuously and happens to everyone. We take in information and construct our meaning of it, and we do so over and over again. Because learning is seen as occurring in this way, the primary teaching tasks of schools and teachers are (1) to provide constructivist-rich learning experiences, (2) to stimulate and guide learner constructivist thinking, and (3) to remember continuously that all members of the community—students, teachers, staff members, administrators, and parents—are learning all the time. Particularly important is the realization that teachers continuously learn from and about students just as students learn from teachers. According to Dewey (1916/1944), the student is both student and teacher and the teacher is both teacher and student, and the less obvious the role distinctions are to each the better the educative experience (p. 160).

Learning and the School Community

Because learning is continuous and always happening to everyone, everyone in a school community has the chance to be simultaneously a learner and a teacher, and everyone has the responsibility for doing so. Mathematics is not really learned in only one classroom and English in another. The proper behavior of a group of students is not the exclusive domain of the one teacher to whom that group is assigned. Teachers are not the only creators of learning. Students learn from each other and from cafeteria workers, secretaries, and custodians. Everyone learns because they live in, and therefore experience, the learning environment.

When this pervasive type of learning occurs, community members accept shared values, purposes, and commitments tied to a mission of learning, and that sense of mission bonds them to each other and to their shared work. They enjoy positive interpersonal relationships and shared roles and responsibilities. They possess a sense of connectedness and belonging that includes everyone. They view the school community more as a tightly knit neighborhood or an extended family than as a production line or a delivery system.

This pervasive nature of learning also ties directly to the view of schools and learning as morally good and virtuous. In learning community schools, students consider their learning to be desirable and teachers value student learning to such an extent that they identify successful student learning as the most important intrinsic reward they seek. Scholars have told us for years that human inquisitiveness, a desire to explore, and a need to make sense out of things (to figure things out) stimulate and channel human energy to learn; school communities built around the creation of learning experiences capitalize on this inquisitiveness. They celebrate learning as the constant and righteous mission of the school, not only in a general and abstract way but also in ways that guide every teaching decision and every learning activity.

When learning is clearly recognized as the school's mission and learning experiences are firmly established as the primary focus of school energy (rather than the measurement of the results of learning), teachers can concentrate on creating learning experiences rather than on testing their apparent results and students can more freely inquire, explore, figure things out, ask their own questions, discover for themselves, and develop their thinking skills. Classrooms and schools can be thought of as busy, action-oriented, intellectual, and work-centered environments. Learning becomes both the school's mission and a schoolwide norm. Everyone seeks it; everyone does it; and everyone has fun doing so.

When school leaders do not think of learning as experience-based intellectual construction and do not build school communities around a central moral purpose of creating learning experiences for students, they miss the opportunity of using the goodness of learning as the reason why they exist, as justification for what they do, and as motivation to sustain their work. When this happens, they seem to be forced to turn to some form of comparative, measured results of learning instead of to learning itself as evidence and justification of their worthiness. They search for indicators of success by comparing achievement scores between students, teachers' classes, schools, and school systems rather than by comparing what individual students know, can do, and believe today and what they knew, could do, and believed a few days ago. Their evidence of success becomes having higher test scores in comparison with those of someone else.

Focusing on comparative achievement overemphasizes competition, self-interest, and human selfishness and undervalues personal inquisitiveness, self-satisfaction, and the intrinsic motivation and excitement of learning. It substitutes in learners' minds a desire to get ahead of someone else for the desire to learn more. Schools become so caught up in the competition for external rewards and getting ahead of others that they lose sight of the rewards of learning itself.

CHAPTER THREE

Revisioning Teaching and Professional Growth

*How should we describe teaching and learning
to teach as professional learning community
experiences?*

In this chapter, we describe different ways of looking at what teachers do as they engage in their professional work and how and what they learn as they learn to teach. First, we present a view of teaching that we label *teaching as professional practice*; then we explain an alternative view of teacher learning that is embedded in professional practice. These two remaining dimensions of our vision of learning community schools extend the ideas presented in Chapter 2. Although this chapter is divided into two parts—one on the nature of teaching and a second on the nature of teacher learning—the ideas presented overlap because a major point in our thinking is that teaching and learning to teach are not separate processes.

When we think of schools as learning communities and learning as a continuous, lifelong, experience-based process of intellectual construction, we need to think differently about teaching, how teachers learn to teach, and what teachers need to know and to be able to do. In this context, teaching is more complex than the delivery of ideas, skills, and value perspectives to students, more than the implementation of teacher ideas and beginning skills learned in preservice education and then applied in class after class and with student after student, and more than a routine process or sets of processes taught to beginning professionals and then repeated year after year with slight fine-tuning until they are done "right." The process starts with what Dan Lortie (1975) calls "the apprenticeship of observation," where those who become teachers are classroom students; it evolves through a professional career of classroom practice; and it ends (as mentioned in Chapter 1) at retirement or later (Leithwood, 1992). (Here, again, John Holt's [Canfield & Hansen, 1993] image of learning to play and playing the cello fits.)

Teaching as Professional Practice

Our idea of teaching professionals is that of investigative, executive-type, decision-making, managing, and performing experts who are intelligent, knowledgeable, skilled, morally sound, sensitive, thinking, inquiring, and continuous learners. These professionals are more than born artists who care for children, more than master craftspersons who teach as they have seen others teach and as they were trained to teach, and more than assembly line workers who perform routine tasks as they are told. Although characteristics of the artist, the craftsperson, and the assembly line worker exist in what teachers do, the essence of teachers' professional work is both intellectual and investigative, and these two characteristics combine in ways that make teaching different from the work of others. Teachers rely on more than their natural talents, their compassion for children, and that which training, common sense, personal trial and error, and hunch tell them. They do more than follow routines, and more than apply the ideas and techniques that they remember from their schooling, from their college coursework, and from what worked in prior years and with former students. They have to do more than like the subject matter they teach, love children, and tell the students what they need to know.

Teachers perform the most complex and most prized work of schools. Because their work is why schools exist, they form the core of the school community. In fact, their knowledge, multiple skills, values, and commitments largely determine whether schools are good and whether students learn as much as they should. And all this happens while schools, teaching, society, and the lives of students change at rapidly increasing paces and in ever-expanding ways.

Beginning teachers simply cannot know all they need to know and do not have all the competencies and value perspectives that they need to have to teach really well. They cannot arrive at the door of their first classroom as prepackaged experts, fully informed and filled with

finely honed skills and clearly understood values. To expect them to
be completely mature professionally at the start of their careers is both
unrealistic and naive. Their previous learning has gotten them to the
point at which they know enough and can do some things well enough
to start teaching students, but they have a professional lifetime of
learning ahead of them.

After teachers' initial preservice study, much of what they learn is
learned by teaching and from teaching. Each experience—with a lesson, a class, an individual student, a professional colleague, an admin-
istrator, a parent—is logged in intellectually into a teacher's conceptual framework and built into his or her personalized professional set
of knowledge, skills, and values. As this happens, teachers (like all
learners) inquire, explore, discover, figure things out, test hypotheses,
and decide what is best for their own teaching and their own students
(Simpson & Jackson, 1997). In the process, they reap the intrinsic rewards that accompany learning as well as the rewards that accrue, at
least potentially, from their improved teaching.

Teachers as Learning Practitioners

Because teachers continuously learn from their teaching, we
prefer to use *teacher learning* instead of the terms *teacher education*
and *professional development,* and we characterize what teachers do
as *professional practice.* We think both teacher learning and professional practice fit better the idea of teaching as a never-ending process
of investigating and experimenting, reflecting and analyzing what one
does in the classroom and school, formulating one's own personal
professional theories and using these theories to guide future practice,
and deciding what and how to teach based on one's best personal
professional judgment (Eraut, 1994; Schön, 1987).

Thinking of teaching in this constructivist way blurs the distinction
between preservice and in-service education, research and practice,
research-based knowledge and practice-level knowledge, and doing
teaching and studying what teachers do. It questions the assumptions
that the primary way novice teachers learn is from watching, listening
to, and mimicking more experienced teachers who developed their
expertise in the same way some years earlier and have arrived at the
point of having completed their learning. It also challenges the notions
that there are exemplars of teaching that constitute best practice for
all situations and that competent bureaucratically designated in-

structional leaders can and should direct teachers how to teach their students.

Learning community schools recognize that teacher learning is constructivist, self-motivated, and continuous. They think of teacher learning on the job as a normal and integral part of what teachers do—a process that starts early in every teacher's life and never stops. Therefore, in-service teacher education is not something that has to be done to teachers in need of remediation. It is educative and broadening rather than deficit reducing. It does not blame teachers for not already knowing something; it helps teachers build on what they already know and can do. It contrasts sharply with a more common approach to teacher in-service education that is often described in ways similar to the following: School system administrators and supervisors conduct workshops in which they supply to teachers information about new approaches to teaching and new curriculum packages, things that school and district leaders have learned about but presumably teachers have not. They explain these "new and better" approaches and packages, tell teachers to try them, and assume that the teachers will take these new ways of doing things to their classroom and apply them in their teaching. Then they closely supervise what the teachers do to be sure they apply them properly. Sometimes, artificial rewards in the form of extra pay and special recognition are provided.

Teachers who are career-long professional practitioners lead learner-centered, inquiring communities, and they learn as they lead. Instead of positioning themselves above a learning process that they devise and manipulate just for students, they, along with their students, engage in analysis, reflection, problem solving, and critical thinking; and they do so in an intellectual atmosphere of respect, trust, openness, and investigation. As they encourage, guide, facilitate, and manage student learning, they actively participate in that learning. As a result, they get better at both learning and teaching (Myers, 1996b, 1997a).

As experienced-based, investigative, constructivist learners, teachers come to school each day to explore, inquire, think, develop professionally, and become better at teaching. They come to teach and to learn to teach.

When this attitude is a norm for a school, the school is a real learning community. All members learn, continue to develop, and get better at what they do. As they do this, they build into the community's culture the capacity for continuous learning and the expectation that it occurs automatically. Every community member is a participating learner—and teacher.

In this learning atmosphere, leadership status is assigned to people who demonstrate intellectual insight and curiosity, professional inquisitiveness, honest self-study, pedagogical effectiveness, commitment to improvement, and collegial helpfulness, rather than to those who hold hierarchical positions, have long terms of service, have accumulated large amounts of personal knowledge, or have developed individual expertise. Relationships develop around fulfilling the community's moral purpose of enhanced learning. Every student's learning and every teacher's continuing professional learning are central, communitywide responsibilities (Barth, 1990; Eraut, 1994; Lambert et al., 1995, 1997; Prawat, 1992; Sergiovanni, 1992, 1996).

Despite this view of teacher learning, many educators, including teachers, still see teacher professional learning as gathering finite packages of ideas, skills, value orientations, and tricks of the trade and using them routinely and ever more skillfully year after year. The thinking proceeds somewhat like this: Preservice teacher education supplies teachers with their theoretical ideas; life experiences and common sense add more information; student teaching and the first 2 or 3 years on the job provide practical ideas and practice; in-service education fills in ideas, skills, and perspectives missed along the way and adds periodic updates; and trial and error and professional wisdom gained from experience supply whatever else teachers need. Such thinking considers schools as places where teachers deliver instructions by applying knowledge they have already learned about teaching, using skills they have already fully developed, and imposing value perspectives they have already personally formulated to perfection (Little, 1982, 1990, 1993; Little et al., 1987). Even centuries ago, Geoffrey Chaucer knew better than this when, in *The Canterbury Tales,* he said of his teacher, "Gladly would he learn, and gladly teach."

Schools as Centers of Teacher Learning

The intellectual atmosphere of learning community schools enhances, sustains, and guides teacher professional learning as an integral element of its reason for being—as part of its moral purpose. The reasons for this are rather simple: Schools exist to create student learning; teachers are the primary professionals who do this; if student learning is to be as good as it can be, teaching needs to be just as good;

therefore, schools need to build into their goals, priorities, and activities an increasing capacity for teachers to get better at what they do.

In our vision, learning community schools assume this responsibility for helping teachers get better, the community environment provides the intellectual setting for professional learning to occur, the goal of improved student learning supplies the motivation and justification for teachers to improve their practice, and teachers themselves provide the leadership for getting better. In this setting, teacher professional activities such as in-class experimentation, schoolwide analysis of strengths and weaknesses, cooperation, and collegial collaboration constitute much of the actual learning. School administrators, consultants, and college professors add assistance, information, resources, and support to the learning endeavor. When all this happens with some degree of synchronization, teacher learning becomes a self-sustaining school community activity and goal.

Teachers who teach in this environment and all community participants assume that their school will continually improve because they will improve as individuals and as a professional unit. This assumption, in turn, provides built-in expectations and capacities for ongoing change and adaptation. Teachers do not have to find extra time to do this, and they do not risk failure in front of their peers when their experiments do not succeed. The professional norms assure everyone that experimentation, investigation, and analysis are all parts of what is done to improve teaching and create better student learning. The ideas that teachers have to be "in-serviced" and forced by administrators to change become anachronisms and are considered insulting to professionals.

Because norms such as these are in place, teachers who do not attempt to improve their practice and do not constantly experiment, reflect on, analyze, and modify their teaching are the ones who become uncomfortable and feel out of place. The professional learning climate, the getting-better agendas, and the successes of their colleagues force them to convert or leave. In a true professional community, that is as it should be.

This scenario, of course, does not describe the way in which most schools currently operate, a point reflected bluntly in teachers' typical assessments of the professional development practices to which they are exposed. In short, most teachers now rate their in-service professional development activities as irrelevant, nonintellectual, and boring; they frequently make similar judgments about continuing teacher education courses (Eraut, 1994; Little, 1983, 1992, 1993; Little et al., 1987; Lortie, 1975, pp. 76-77; Shanker, 1990).

Other Professionals Provide Support

Although making teacher learning a central school community activity and goal may seem to many a matter of common sense, changing from today's typical pattern of teacher in-service education is not an easy task. Doing so requires modifications in how teachers, administrators, and teacher educators think about both teaching and learning and about their various professional roles. It involves changes in who is in charge, how teachers' time is used, and how school money is spent. It requires significant reconfigurations of relationships among teachers, between teachers and administrators, between individual schools and the wider school system in which they operate, and between all the above and college-based teacher educators. It means centering professional development in the study of teaching practice, focusing it on improving student learning, and conducting it within the teachers' normal work day and primarily at the school site. Teachers become the leaders, whereas others—administrators, consultants, and college-based teacher educators—respond to teacher requests and serve as their coaches and advisors. In essence, these other professionals become reactors, resources, and aides to teachers instead of their directors and superiors (Barth, 1990; Isaacson & Bamburg, 1992; Lambert et al., 1995, 1997).

In this setting, teacher professional development is tied directly to what teachers need to know and be able to do to teach their students better and what they learn in and from their teaching, instead of being tied to new curriculum packages or teaching ideas that someone thinks ought to be taught to teachers; and the contributions of administrators, consultants, and college-based teacher educators are tied directly to how well they help teachers improve their teaching with their students. The importance of nonclassroom-teacher professionals is judged by how helpful they are to teachers, how crucial they are to the school's operation, and how much personal stake and commitment they have invested in the students, the teachers, and the school's success. If they are outsiders who deliver only ideas and resources developed elsewhere or they are perceived in this way, their roles are marginal. If, on the other hand, they are seen and see themselves as true community members—true participants and true stakeholders—

they have central, larger, and more critical roles to play and much work to do.

It is, of course, in the interest of school communities to draw into their membership all the potentially helpful experts who can make contributions and play central parts in the communities' work—college-based experts, parents, other community resource people, and so forth. Their expertise can provide teachers with the knowledge, skills, perspectives, insights, encouragement, resources, and support they need for their own learning and that of their students. Good learning communities make maximum use of these experts and, in the process, draw them into community membership so closely that they identify personally with the community and its goals and work. When this happens, the experts share personally in the community's successes and failures, accept responsibility for achieving its mission, and contribute to everyone's learning, including their own. They look for ways to help, rather than stand outside and criticize.

Teaching as Investigative Problem Identification and Problem Solving

When we think of teaching as professional practice, the act of classroom teaching can be described (as mentioned in Chapter 1) as two successive teacher tasks: (1) figuring out ways in which to educate the students for whom a teacher is responsible, and (2) trying in the classroom what the teacher thinks will work. To the extent that any particular strategy works, the teaching creates the desired student learning and is, therefore, successful. But teaching is never totally successful, and at any given time a student's learning is never complete. Therefore, teachers always have to study what they do and think of better, different, and newer ways of reaching students. They need to do so for every student, every class, every day, in every subject. The process sounds like a big task with many parts, and it is, but it is not impossible. In fact, it occurs to some extent naturally for any intellectually sophisticated teacher. The process is investigative problem identification and problem solving, a natural part of the teacher's constructivist learning.

As teachers problem solve in a constructivist way, they construct new meaning and use the new ideas to interpret future observations and events. For example, when a third-grade teacher tries to teach a mathematics lesson on division with remainders and nearly no student grasps the idea, or a high school history teacher tries to teach 18th-century rationalism and the students stare blankly as if he or she had been speaking in Greek, the lessons in one sense have not failed; they simply have been tried and have not yet succeeded under certain conditions and with particular individuals. In either case, the teachers' problems of creating the desired student learning have not yet been solved. But in the process, the teachers have learned something about their teaching, about their students, and about themselves, even if that something is the fact that they now know one more way of teaching that does not work for them under a particular set of circumstances.

A medical professional's work can serve as an illustrative analogy. When a person with an unexplained allergic skin reaction visits an allergist's office, the physician often tries to diagnose the problem by applying different potentially reaction-producing substances to the patient's skin. If the first application does not identify the cause of the allergic reaction, neither the doctor nor the patient assumes that the physician has failed; they just try the next substance. The process is not simply unguided trial and error, of course, and more knowledgeable and more experienced allergists can be expected to identify the correct cause of the problem more quickly because they have learned more and experienced more similar conditions. But immediate cures are not usually assured, especially if there are many unusual aspects of the patient's health condition that the physician does not know about or has not seen before. And different patients, like students, respond differently to the same treatment. The allergist in this illustration is a problem solver, and he or she both uses present knowledge to attack the problem and gains new knowledge from doing so. The physician's expertise builds with each new medical problem he or she confronts.

We acknowledge that teaching today is only rarely looked at as problem identification and problem solving in this way. Instead, teachers are supposed to know the answers and supply students with what they need as if the students are receptacles ready to be filled and all their learning needs are similar, if not the same. Such thinking is simplistic but nonetheless pervasive. More important, the thinking is detrimental to improving teaching practice. It sends teachers to manuals, workshops, and college courses for solutions to their teaching problems when closer, more analytical study, experimentation, and reflection on what does and does not work with individual students and classes could be just as productive, or more so.

Teachers who see themselves as investigative problem identifiers and problem solvers, who view their own and their students' learning as intellectual constructivism, and who teach in an atmosphere of inquiry naturally and constantly examine their work and its results. Their mission is to create learning opportunities for students, and they hold themselves accountable for doing so. They keep trying to solve the multiple problems before them in the persons of every student in their classes and in terms of what each of those students needs to know and be able to do. They do not expect to meet every need of all students on each occasion, but they do expect to tackle a manageable number of the problems at a time, to solve some of them, and to get better at doing so year after year.

When teaching is thought of as investigative problem identification and problem solving, teachers base their efforts at improving their practice on close-up looks at what they are doing with their students and how well it is paying off. They do this not as isolated individuals but as members of a professional culture that values inquiry, collegial collaboration, and mutual learning. Their investigations are not simple efforts at trial and error (Barth, 1990; Myers, 1995a, 1996b; Sergiovanni, 1992, 1996). They are analyses that lead to theories generated from practice that can inform colleagues and the profession at large. How this analysis and theory building occurs is explained below.

Analyzing Practice as a Starting Point

Because teachers interact with individual students up close every day, they are, in fact, front-line experts. They are the professionals closest to the scene of action—where the student learning occurs—and, as a result, they are the best informed about individual students and classes, the school context, and their own teaching strengths, weaknesses, successes, and failures. They know best what happened yesterday and what to expect for tomorrow. They know better than anyone else what works for them with their own students.

Therefore, a logical starting point for teachers who want to increase their understanding of both teaching and learning and improve their professional practice is to examine their classroom work personally and then reflect on and assess it (Eraut, 1994; Prawat, 1992; Schön, 1987). Teachers who do this can make judgments about how well their students are learning and whether that learning is consistent with their instructional goals. They can also decide whether to make changes in their teaching, and, if so, how to implement them.

Improving teaching and student learning by starting with teachers analyzing their classroom practice, however, differs in three important ways from the ways in which teacher professional development and school change are now typically understood. First, it assumes that teachers are the appropriate instructional leaders and change agents of a school and that principals and supervisors (consultants would be a better title) are there to respond to their needs by providing resources, support, advice, feedback, and assistance, rather than dictating direction and devising in-service education activities. Second, it assumes that teachers see self-analysis, reflection, and personal professional development as normal components of the task of teaching and they are competent to handle their personal responsibilities for this learning along with their day-to-day work with students. Third, it assumes that what teachers need to know and to be able to do to improve their teaching is derived primarily from their problem-solving efforts.

It also avoids some of the biggest weaknesses of the deficit model of teacher development by taking full advantage of teacher expertise and needs, their values and beliefs about their work, the body of practice-based ideas and skills they have developed from their own practice, their personal views of themselves, their aspirations, their general outlook on life, their individual stages of development, and their attachments to their school and its mission. It places a high value on the people, practices, ideas, and circumstances already in place in the school—the local context in which change is being undertaken.

A Culture of Inquiry

That local school context is critical. In every school, teachers teach within a work culture that has been built up over time and is a product of an intricate web of shared values, norms of behavior, personal relationships, and perceived individual strengths and weaknesses. That work culture is unique to each school community. It influences how things are usually done in the school, who does what, and how people feel about what they do and about each other. Any attempt to change how things are done in a school, including attempts to reform, restructure, and have teachers teach differently, is mediated, interpreted, and realized through that work culture (Sikes, 1992).

Within the work culture is an element that some researchers call an "ethic of practicality" (Doyle & Ponder, 1977). Because of this ethic, teachers who are asked to change their practice base their decisions on the usefulness of the proposed change for their teaching, its congruence with their view of correct practice, and the ease with which they believe they can implement it. Unless the idea is deemed by teachers to be useful, relevant, and practical rather than unproven, abstract, and theoretical, it is not likely to be accepted. Therefore, ideas generated outside the local school context and delivered to teachers as one year's cure for inadequate student learning and less-than-satisfactory teaching are met almost instantly with skepticism and resistance. They are typically viewed as intrusions into the current good work of teachers and burdens requiring efforts that distract teachers from their mission. The "outsiders" who push them are considered to be inadequately informed about the teachers' professional knowledge and skills and inattentive to local circumstances and needs.

Because of the work culture in place in any school community and because of that culture's emphasis on an ethic of practicality, one wonders why efforts intended to help teachers teach better ever start with predetermined ideas of outsiders about what teachers need and how they should change. They should start instead with the ideas and needs of the teachers as perceived by the teachers themselves. This means that reformers, restructurers, staff developers, and university-school partners should not approach teachers with a "look-what-I-have-for-you" attitude. Instead, they should ask, What do you need? How can I help you accomplish what you want?

We realize that when teachers are asked the what-do-you-need question, they often indicate that they do not know what they need. But we do not believe this is an invitation for outsiders to tell them what they need. It is, instead, evidence that helping them find out what they need is a legitimate starting point. It also suggests that they are not accustomed to being asked what they need and to being expected to think probingly for themselves and about themselves. It means that an honest finding-out process is the appropriate first step to getting better (Nadler, 1986). We say "honest" because the process of identifying teacher needs cannot be an exercise in manipulation. It must be educative and start with teachers inquiring into their practice, not with an acceptance of a pat answer or a selection from off-the-shelf innovations that may or may not fit. The goal is to improve teaching through teacher learning, not to adopt something new as a cure-all or for the sake of change.

It is a mistake to think of teachers as practitioners who do routine, unchanging work in a culture that values doing the same thing year after year. Teachers should instead be thought of as professionals who constantly inquire into their practice, constantly think about what and how they teach, constantly investigate, and constantly experiment and assess the results of their trial efforts. This way of looking at teachers as inquirers combines the teaching of students and the learning of teachers and it places teachers in charge of improving their own practice. It perceives teaching as an intellectual self-renewing endeavor and therefore school change as an ongoing process of educational renewal, a renewal that is genuinely educational and educative. Teachers constantly seek to get better at their practice because of their commitment to student learning and because they sincerely want to be as good at their profession as they can be. They seek new ideas and more refined skills not for their own sake or to please administrators, but because the ideas and skills inform and improve their practice. They decide if, when, and how to use new information and different teaching techniques based on how useful those techniques are in helping them teach individual students and specific classes of students better. Better teaching and better student learning are both their goals and their mission (see Goodlad, 1994a).

Collegial Relationships and Teacher Learning

When teachers inquire into their practice as members of learning communities, they do not do so in isolation from their colleagues or while working alone with their own students. To do so individually and in isolation runs counter to the school learning community atmosphere and misses the mutually reinforcing learning of group study among professionals. Just as teachers who teach with collegial interaction and mutual interdependence teach better, teachers who study their teaching together learn more about their own and their colleagues' teaching, and they do so more analytically, more insightfully, and more metacognitively (Barth, 1990; Fullan, 1993; Lambert et al., 1995, 1997; Myers, 1995b, 1997a).

In learning community schools, teachers share a common school purpose—a desire to educate all students—and that purpose involves an acceptance by every teacher of a responsibility for improving the teaching of every other teacher throughout the school, a sense of mutual caring for each other, and a commitment to help one another succeed. Teachers forge friendly interpersonal professional relationships, talk with one another about their work, sympathize, congratulate, offer suggestions, and develop consensus. Over time, their interpersonal relationships develop into mutual loyalty, trust, and commitment. Because of this commitment to each other as well as to their common cause, the teachers evolve from a cluster of individuals who happen to teach in the same building into a team of interdependent professionals—a community of educators, gladly teaching and gladly learning together (Barth, 1990; Little et al., 1987; Rosenholtz, 1989).

Researchers refer to this combination of commitments, relationships, and caring as a special attitude, orientation, and norm that they label *collegiality,* and they suggest that collegiality enables a number of good things to happen in schools. For example, Judith Warren Little et al. (1987) say that teacher collaborative work enables teachers to attempt curricular and instructional innovations that they would probably not have tried individually, and that teachers who collaborate are more likely to visit each others' classes, observe each other teach, and study classroom-related issues together. Susan Rosenholtz (1989) observes, in her comparison of learning-enriched and learning-impoverished schools, that

> the extent to which teachers share instructional goals also contributes independently to their opportunities for learning. . . . Teacher collaboration is the final predictor of teachers' learning opportunities, independent of all others. Learning may be the direct outcome of collaboration, as teachers request from, and offer colleagues, new ideas, strategies, and techniques. But quite apart from the rendering of technical assistance, collaboration may indirectly influence learning through the leadership of teachers within the school. Teacher leaders' enthusiasm for experimentation . . . has a contagious quality. The pedagogical appeal of such energetic locomotion seems almost irresistible in inducing others to share, to experiment, and to grow. (p. 78)

It is important to recognize that collegiality among teachers is more than just cooperation and teamwork. It is a trust-level working together that includes a deep-seated and strongly held professional commitment to one another. Key elements include personal closeness, mutual caring, and professional interdependence. Colleagues do special things for others whom they know, like, and trust. They tackle shared problems more willingly and more openly. They need the assurance that their trust is justified (Grimmett & Crehan, 1992; Hargreaves & Dawe, 1990; Sergiovanni, 1992). Some writers call collegiality a bonding experience; Sergiovanni (1992, 1994, 1996) calls it covenantal and spiritual. Whatever the phenomenon is called, in learning communities colleagues trust and have faith in each other. They count on each others' competence, loyalty, and advice and they are vulnerable if betrayed.

Different Intellectual Norms

Collegiality as we are describing it rests on different intellectual norms than those present in most schools today and transforms how teachers conduct their work. It makes teaching a public learning endeavor among professionals rather than something secret in the private domains of individuals who hide their work behind closed classroom doors. It requires an openness to professional scrutiny, and that scrutiny breeds interdependence, interpersonal support and influence, and mutual respect (see Little, 1987, p. 496). It helps teacher learning because of its pooling of ideas and advice, its sharing of burdens, and its recognition of performance.

When teachers function collegially, they seem to engage in their teaching more deeply, more intellectually, and more analytically. They think about what they do more often and more probingly. They ask colleagues for opinions, feedback, and critiques, and they are more prone to offer the same. They are more inquiring about their work and more willing to admit mistakes and make changes. They watch each other and strive to be as good as their best colleagues. They realize that each member of the team has different talents and specialties, and they try to maximize each person's contributions. They reinforce each others' high expectations and work hard to reach them. They also help their professional friends be as good as they can be, and are so helped in return.

This intellectual aspect of collegiality among teachers builds and sustains an inquiring, learning culture among professionals (Lieberman, 1989), one that reinforces a collective desire to get better at teaching. As teachers talk about their work, compare their ideas and practices, and develop a professional language, they raise questions such as, What do you do when that happens? Do you get the results you want?

What would happen if I did the same thing? Where can we find more data? If I try it, will you tell me what you think? Will you help me do this with my students?

When collegiality and a professional learning atmosphere become norms among teachers, a continuously reinforcing cycle develops. Teachers engage in collegial interdependence and experimentation, which increases their ability to take risks even if these risks threaten self-esteem; that willingness to experiment and take risks makes teachers more open to feedback, criticism, and advice; the openness enables them to learn more and change more easily (see Elliott, 1988). All this causes teachers to ask fundamental questions about the nature of teaching and student learning. That questioning changes teachers' perceptions of teaching—from a profession that has set ways of doing things learned first and applied later to a profession that includes learning as a central and continuing component of the practice.

Although collegiality among teachers can be stimulated, reinforced, and enhanced by administrative leaders and through efforts at school restructuring, it is not likely to develop to its fullest unless it grows from the hearts, minds, and professional motivations of teachers themselves and is sustained by these motives (Grimmett & Crehan, 1992; Hargreaves & Dawe, 1990). These motives depend heavily on how teachers conceive of their professional work—how willing they are to admit that they are learners about teaching as well as doers of teaching and how secure they feel as practitioners in their school community. In learning community schools, teachers see the value of collegial practices in helping them teach better and enabling them to feel better about their teaching. Getting better is something they are expected to do and they expect of themselves. It is rooted securely in the beliefs and values of their school community.

Collegiality as an element in teacher learning is therefore a recognized and celebrated part of a school community's normal way of life. It is the expected and comfortable way for teachers to conduct business. It helps teachers discover how to teach better, provides them with guidance as they try new things, and supplies them with the security of knowing they are not alone.

Teachers who practice their profession collegially are collectively their own managers, their own experts, and their own decision makers. They commit to work together because they believe doing so results in improved student learning. They know what they want to accomplish and believe in what they do. They are secure in what they do but they know that they can do better and, therefore, assess and evaluate their own and their colleagues' work, learn by doing so, and adjust their practice. They recognize their individual and collective strengths, weaknesses, and talents; they build on the strengths and bridge the weaknesses; and they are better as a group because of doing so. They have high expectations of each other and themselves; they rely on each other and know that others rely on them. They work hard and can expect everyone else to be just as hardworking. They take pride in what they learn collectively.

Theories Generated in Practice

When teachers inquire into and analyze their own practice effectively, they do more than decide on a trial-and-error level which specific things do or do not work. They formulate general principles— *principles of practice*—about what and how to teach, and they use these general ideas in an experimental way to guide their future work. As they engage in the problem-identifying and problem-solving tasks described earlier, they pursue a sequence somewhat like this: (1) gather knowledge about teaching from all sources, including from their personal teaching; (2) formulate that knowledge into hypotheses; (3) test the hypotheses by using them in classes and watch colleagues do the same; and (4) assess the results. The process continues day after day, and with each trial the hypotheses are adjusted and refined. When this happens, the hypotheses become more useful and more widely applicable, and therefore more valid. As the problem-solving teachers share their ideas and experiences with colleagues, the colleagues test the hypotheses in their own classrooms as well and thereby expand the hypotheses' testing arena. At some point, the refined hypotheses become accepted so widely and so convincingly that professional practitioners come to consider them general norms of practice—the way good teachers do things. We call them *practice-based theories* because underlying each are teacher-developed philosophies of teaching and learning (see Eraut, 1984; Schön, 1983, 1987).

Teachers as Scholar Practitioners

When this happens, teachers are in fact the scholar practitioners that Robert Schaefer (1967) hoped for when he wrote in the 1960s. They are students and investigators of their own practice. They are inquiring thinkers about teaching in addition to skilled doers in a technical sense. They create knowledge about teaching and learning, just as researchers on teaching do. They are not just users of knowledge developed elsewhere and distributed to them by a university researcher or someone higher on an administrative chain of command. Instead, they convert schools from places where knowledge, skills, and value perspectives are used to centers where knowledge, skills, and value perspectives are also generated and formulated—to centers of inquiry.

We acknowledge that our ideas of scholar-practitioner teachers and practice-based theory assume expertise on the part of teachers and an authority possessed by teachers over their work not normally present in schools today. In many schools, little time or encouragement is available for teachers to study their own practice, and although supervisors and principals evaluate teacher performances, they rarely study them in an attempt to learn from them. They only infrequently help disseminate a practice-based good idea from one teacher to others. In fact, they often do not recognize the usefulness of teacher-developed ideas and do not see a disseminator function of this type among their roles. At the same time, many teachers do not see themselves as students of teaching or as developers of ideas useful to the general profession. They still think of themselves simply as artisans. They give suggestions and advice to beginners but try not to "push" their ideas on those who are equally experienced. They look down on "boastful" colleagues and they avoid asking for advice from others. If they "borrow" professional ideas from colleagues, they frequently do so surreptitiously, with anxiety and guilt. They often fear being viewed as uninformed or less skilled (Glidewell, Tucker, Todt, & Cox, 1983).

When teaching is conceived of as professional practice and teachers are thought of as scholar practitioners, however, teachers use their classroom experimentation, experience, reflection, and analysis to develop general principles and theories of practice. These then evolve into intellectual tools that have the potential of guiding teaching practice across classrooms and schools. Because the process includes theory building, it is neither trial-and-error in nature nor limited to specific settings. And although it rises from particular teachers' personal classroom experiences, it also relies on the experimenting teachers' previously learned knowledge and competence, ideas that they draw on from all sources, and the assessments, reflection, and modifications supplied to them by other scholar practitioners.

More Than Action Research

Many educators label the phenomenon we have been describing as *action research,* and it might be appropriate to do so. But we have reservations about using this term for two reasons. First, action research seems to us to imply an inferiority to pure research or scholarly research, which some believe comes only from controlled studies, research-focused investigations, and scholarly tracts. Second, action research is often thought of as applying to a specific situation theories formulated elsewhere. We think theories about teaching and learning can be generated in and generalized from practice as well as from scholarly research projects and controlled studies, and we think both types of theory building are equally worthy of passing on for broad, professionwide use (Eraut, 1994).

In making this point, we are reminded of a story about a dentist who noticed that a group of his patients living in a certain area had particularly discolored teeth yet almost never experienced tooth decay. He decided to investigate, and he believed that doing so was a legitimate part of his work as a dentist. We all know the outcome of his practice-based research and inquiry: It was this dentist who discovered the tooth-protecting benefits of fluoride.

As they search for the best ways to teach each year's group of students, teachers investigate classroom phenomena all the time. Doing so is a normal function of their teaching. But little of this searching leads to broadly applied theories that will help teachers and students, including those at great distances from the school in which particular teacher investigators teach. The influence is much more limited because many teachers attack their classroom problems narrowly, as if the problems are unique to their classroom and their students. They do not see themselves as the scholar practitioners that Schaefer (1967) and Dewey (1916/1944) had in mind so long ago.

In spite of this narrow approach, however, good teachers are scholar practitioners even if they do not think of themselves as such and are not typically recognized as such, and even if the investigative parts of their work are usually submerged from outsider view. In learning community schools, this scholar-practitioner aspect of teaching is raised to a prominent level, encouraged more noticeably, rewarded more often, and provided for in the time and space of teachers' work. Teachers conduct investigations collaboratively and systematically instead of just swapping stories of trial-and-error experiences. They study jointly what seems to work with one class and not another, then extend their successful ideas from teacher to teacher, school to school, and system to system. They pass on specific teaching techniques informally to close colleagues, who then replicate them. Together they develop more fundamental principles that explain more deeply why certain efforts succeed and others do not. Once they form answers to these "why" questions, they communicate their new understanding to the profession at large, including college-based teacher educators and more traditional researchers.

When this happens, more is involved than the developing of better or easier means of communication among teachers. The nature and depth of what teachers discuss and think about changes. They question, probe, reflect on, and ponder more. They develop more responsibility for finding better ways to help students learn and take on a great obligation to improve teaching at large—as a profession. They see their work with students from an additional perspective—as a beginning point for improving student learning, not just for their own students but for students everywhere. They see themselves as knowledge creators, not just consumers, as informers of the practice, not just those who are informed by more knowledgeable others. They have a different attitude about teaching and what it entails. They see themselves as teacher educators as well as teachers.

These changes in perception and attitude help make all teachers' classroom work a professional learning experience in a constructivist sense and they make their inquiry into their work a metacognitive-level intellectual exercise (Lambert et al., 1997). Teachers not only develop new ideas about teaching, they also study how they develop these ideas. These new perceptions and attitudes transform teachers into scholar practitioners. They make the schools in which these teachers teach learning communities. They improve the quality of both teaching and student learning and they do so continuously.

Professional Knowledge, Competence, and Values

When we think of teaching and learning to teach as the intertwined parallel processes that we have been describing, we also need to think of teacher professional knowledge, competence, and values differently. We need to think of what professional teachers come to know, to be able to do, and to believe as being shaped by both the ways in which teachers learn them and the ways in which teachers put them to use (Eraut, 1994).

In the next few pages, we discuss the nature of teacher professional knowledge, competence, and values from this different perspective—a perspective that is essential for understanding learning community schools. In doing so, we focus on professional knowledge more than on skills and values, but what we describe for professional knowledge also applies to skills and values. We begin by looking at public codified knowledge—the reservoir of general information accumulated by experts over time and available for all those who wish to make use of it. Then we look at the knowledge that teachers generate from their own professional practice and the practice of their colleagues. After that, we discuss how teachers select codified knowledge and merge it with the knowledge they develop from their own and their colleagues' experience, and in doing so we also explain how teachers transform professional knowledge as they learn and use it.

Public Codified Knowledge

Public codified knowledge is a general pool of information that has been gathered and organized by researchers, scholars, thinkers, and everyday people of insight and vision. It stands as a reservoir of publicly known ideas ready to be used by anyone—including teachers—who learns them and finds them valuable. Although the reservoir contains innumerable specific facts, these facts are arranged—codified—into categories and broad abstract principles or theories, such as agreed-on stages of development, styles of learning, or types of learning disabilities, and these categories and general principles help make the knowledge understandable and more readily useful. We explain codified knowledge in some detail in the next few paragraphs because an understanding of the concept is necessary for understanding how teachers use knowledge in their professional practice.

Codified professional teacher knowledge is simply public codified knowledge that applies to teaching and schools—the pool of professional ideas that teachers learn from their professional study—from books, lectures, research reports, and other collected forms of information—rather than from their immediate environment and personal experiences. It makes up much of what is learned in preservice teacher education. It consists of the abstract principles or theories that explain the intellectual phenomena that teachers need to know to teach successfully—the general ideas that teachers turn to as they try to understand each facet of their work and plan lessons and activities. It is often considered the most scholarly form of professional knowledge—the knowledge most worth knowing. For those who think of learning to teach primarily as a process of delivering ideas from theoretical scholars to classroom practitioners—from theory to practice, from thinkers to users—this is the type of knowledge that gets delivered.

Two Dimensions

Codified knowledge is usually organized in two ways or in two dimensions. First, it is often divided into categories, which are frequently labeled *academic disciplines, fields of study,* and *bodies of information*—such as the natural sciences, the social sciences, the humanities, and mathematics. Within each of these divisions are subcategories with labels such as *chemistry, political science, history, literature,* and *calculus.* Second, it is also often separated into levels of abstraction, which are typically referred to as *theories, principles, generalizations, concepts,* and *facts.* The organizing is based on multiple criteria and is done using multiple perspectives. The categories and levels overlap and are complex, confusing at times, and often contradictory, but the groupings that result from the organizing process help make the nature of the knowledge that is grouped more understandable for those who use it because they are able to look at one set of information at a time and to do so from a particular perspective. The groups and labels are more meaningful than multitudes of specific facts (Myers & Myers, 1995, pp. 414-424; Schwab, 1962; Taba, 1962).

In the same way that knowledge is codified to make it more understandable, competencies and values are also codified and organized by category and level of abstraction. For example, competencies can be categorized as intellectual, reading related, physical, manipulative, interpersonal, social, and so forth; and values can be organized in terms of ethics, aesthetics, preferences, and so on (Myers & Myers, 1995, pp. 424-437).

Codified for Particular Purposes

Although the codifying of knowledge, competencies, and values is useful, it is important to remember that any one way of organizing something intellectually is not the only way of doing so. Each way stresses certain perspectives over others. For example, academic disciplines are usually formulated by researchers and scholars in various fields of study, who investigate ideas and then cluster the ideas in ways that fit their purpose, rather than by practical users of the ideas, such as public officials and teachers. Therefore, when teachers use a particular set of ideas for professional purposes, they cannot simply select ideas from the public codified pool without reconfiguring them to fit their specific needs, purposes, and circumstances (Eraut, 1994).

That codified knowledge is organized to fit particular purposes is especially important because many seem to think that when public knowledge is codified and becomes available generally, it takes on an independent existence of its own—it is located somewhere in an intellectual space that is separate from people's minds—as if it rests inertly in a gigantic reservoir separate from thinking people and ready to be tapped in unmodified form for use whenever needed. Although the question of whether or not knowledge exits apart from people's minds is a matter of interesting speculation, it is beyond our purposes here, but nevertheless we must recognize that the appearance that knowledge has an independent existence leads many of us to think of knowledge as a commodity sought out by those who need it and placed into their heads as they learn.

Competencies are also frequently thought of as commodities—as intellectual and physical capabilities that exist in a pool or reservoir somewhere separate from people and ready to be acquired by those who seek to gain possession of them and make them a part of their being. Therefore, competence appears to be something that can be transferred from some other place or passed from one person to another rather than a set of abilities that individuals must develop in their own minds and bodies.

In similar fashion, values are usually thought of as having lives of their own, as entities waiting to be accepted and adopted from without rather than formulated from within. As with knowledge and competence, they are seen as commodities residing in a pool or reservoir waiting to be selected by individuals for their personal use.

Our point here is not to debate either for or against the view that codified knowledge, competencies, and values exist apart from the individual minds and beings that possess them. It is instead to point out that the professional knowledge, competencies, and values that exist in public codified form take on meaning only as they are acquired by teachers and transformed by them into forms that become part of those teachers' individual professional knowledge, competencies, and value systems.

Professional Knowledge

Experts have classified the codified knowledge that teachers draw on for their work as *professional knowledge,* even though there is no clear dividing line between professional knowledge and more general knowledge of other kinds. For example, teachers sometimes find concepts and theories from economics, sociology, political science, and organizational behavior useful in deciding how to handle particular relationships (situations with parents, colleagues, administrators, and school boards) even though these theories were not initially developed to be used in school situations and are not usually thought of in school contexts. Most teachers would not classify them as fitting the label *teacher professional knowledge,* but if teachers use them to serve their professional needs they become, in effect, professional ideas.

In recent years, educational theorists, particularly Lee Shulman (1986), have explained teacher professional knowledge in terms of two general classifications: *pedagogical knowledge*—the professional knowledge that has most to do with how to teach; and *content knowledge*—that which deals primarily with what to teach. Content knowledge is then often subdivided into *subject matter content knowledge, pedagogical content knowledge,* and *curricular knowledge.* Each is described further next.

Pedagogical knowledge includes knowledge about principles of teaching practice—classroom organization and management, methods of instruction, motivation, evaluation; knowledge about schools as organizations and cultures; knowledge of learning and human development; and knowledge often labeled *foundations of education.*

Subject matter content knowledge is the knowledge of subject matter—the concepts and generalizations that make up a discipline plus its syntactic structure—used by teachers to form the student-level content they want their students to learn (Myers & Myers, 1995, pp. 414-424; Schwab, 1962, 1978; Shulman, 1986; Taba, 1962). Although many people equate this type of knowledge with the academic-discipline knowledge of scholars, we take exception with that view. For us, subject matter content knowledge is the knowledge that teachers draw from the disciplines to form the content they want their students to learn—the knowledge that they reconfigure to fit their professional purposes and their students' needs—as well as the subject matter that they use to understand how to do the reconfiguring (Myers & Myers, 1995, pp. 414-424; Shulman, 1986, 1989). Although much of that knowledge is arranged as abstract theories, it is actually available to teachers at all levels of abstraction—from levels as high as the theory, generalization, and conceptual levels that we just discussed to levels as low as very specific facts.

Pedagogical content knowledge is the dimension of subject matter knowledge most germane to being taught to students. It includes not just the subject matter knowledge of disciplinary scholars and other well-informed inquirers in the field but also a large reservoir of the most successful forms of representation of the ideas, the most powerful analogies, illustrations, examples, explanations, and demonstrations that can be used to make the knowledge comprehensible when it is taught to others (Shulman, 1986, 1989). It includes an understanding of what makes student learning of specific topics easy or difficult, how students at different ages are likely to understand and misunderstand ideas, and what instructional techniques are likely to be effective in addressing their misconceptions. This dimension of knowledge, like most knowledge, is developed by teachers from all their learning experiences—formal study, personal life experience, and professional practice (Schulman, 1986, p. 9).

Curricular knowledge is the student-level form of subject matter knowledge arranged as topics and programs to be taught at given grade levels and in suggested sequences. The subject matter after it has been modified and patterned to fit students' learning conditions and needs. In Shulman's (1986) work, it is the "pharmacopeia" of subject matter from which teachers choose that which they teach to students (p. 10).

Acquiring Codified Professional Knowledge

When teachers construct their professional knowledge, they acquire what they need to know to a great extent from the public reservoir of professional codified knowledge because the general concepts and principles in that reservoir provide information about all aspects of their professional work. For example, some of the ideas—in the pedagogical content knowledge category—explain how mathematical content and reading skills should be sequenced to fit students' previous learning and developmental stages; others describe student behavior management techniques most likely to work with certain students and under particular conditions; others suggest which school organization arrangements and which styles of interpersonal interaction usually lead to the most pleasant school environment; and still others indicate which assessment devices are likely to show most validly what students have learned.

But because ideas that reside in the general pool of professional codified knowledge are very broad and abstract—theoretical and conceptual—they cannot be used "off the shelf"; they cannot be simply selected from the pool and slipped unmodified into a specific situation in a teacher's professional practice. They must be understood by the teacher first at the theoretical level, then interpreted, modified, and fit to the particular circumstances and situations in which the teacher wants to use them. For example, Piagetian cognitive-developmental learning theory consists of a body of theoretical principles that explain how children's thinking patterns evolve with their chronological age—children think in certain ways at particular Piagetian developmental stages and differently at other stages. Knowing that set of principles informs teaching practice in general, but teachers must interpret, adjust, and apply that knowledge to specific situations for it to be helpful as they deal with a particular class or student. A third-grade reading teacher can be guided by Piagetian ideas, but those ideas do not supply prescriptions on how to teach reading to a particular class of students.

How and how much teachers modify and reinterpret the codified knowledge they draw on as they solve specific teaching problems varies significantly, depending on many factors—such as the nature of the knowledge the teacher draws on, the way it will be used, and the teacher's personal perceptions, interpretations, and inclinations (Eraut, 1994, pp. 25-58, especially p. 50). If the teacher thinks the fit between the ideas being acquired and the purposes and circumstances where they are to be used is an easy one, the ideas might be replicated relatively intact. If the ideas acquired are compatible but not a neat fit, some degree of modification is in order. If the ideas acquired are useful but substantially different from the setting in which they are to be used, the teacher needs to reinterpret and adjust them to make them work.

Knowledge Constructed From Practice

In addition to acquiring ideas from the public pool of codified professional knowledge, teachers also construct professional knowledge from their own investigative, problem-based teaching in classrooms and their other experiences in schools. The same can be said for professional competencies and values. Some of these practice-based ideas develop into *principles of practice*—guidelines about teaching, students, schools, and teacher activities in general—that evolve as teachers try things, find them successful, repeat them over time, and pass them on to colleagues, who also find them worthy of repeated use. Some such principles, such as specific routines of managing student behavior or teaching language with authentic texts, become so well-known and are accepted so broadly that they become part of the codified pool of professional knowledge. Other ideas that develop in practice, such as particular ways teachers get student attention at the start of class, are more narrowly defined *practice-based propositions*—ideas that are useful in particular types of situations and consistently reliable enough in those settings to be worthy of continued use and replication by others.

A number of scholars who have studied practice-based professional teacher knowledge have described three types—each one defined in terms of the process by which teachers learn the knowledge involved. The types are *technical knowledge, practical* or *craft knowledge,* and *tacit knowledge.* Each is described next.

Technical Knowledge

Technical knowledge is often thought of as the *knowing that* aspect of professional knowledge. Examples include knowing that having clear and well-organized classroom routines and firm student behavior management strategies contribute to the smooth operation of classes; knowing that student attention during recitation lessons can be maintained better by raising questions for the whole class before calling on a specific student. Technical knowledge is acquired from practice throughout teachers' lives—from when preservice teachers are classroom students through preservice professional education courses, and from the first year of teaching until teachers retire. It is not, however, something that has to be learned by every teacher through personal experience. It can be passed on to colleagues by word of mouth, in written form, and through speeches and demonstrations. It can be acquired by teachers in ways separate from their personal teaching practice—for example, through reading in college classes and participating in workshops. It can also be transmitted in the form of principles of practice and can evolve into codified professional knowledge.

Once technical ideas and practices are learned, individual teachers can then apply them to any number of teaching situations where they think they fit. But there is an important difference between possessing technical knowledge and being able to use it well, because using knowledge requires more than becoming aware of an idea or teaching practice at a superficial level. It requires an understanding in some depth and an understanding of when and how to implement it. It also requires a minimum level of competence or skill (e.g., Eraut, 1994; Oakeshott, 1962; Polanyi, 1966, 1969; Ryle, 1949).

Practical or Craft Knowledge

Practical knowledge or craft knowledge, in contrast to technical knowledge, is often described as the *knowing how* aspect of knowledge with emphasis placed on the word *how*. It is the teacher's ability to do something, not just know about it. Examples include knowing how to manage student behavior and knowing how to keep the attention of a full class of students when asking questions that call for individual responses.

Although practical knowledge can be derived from knowledge of all types and from all sources, some people think of it as being learned only by individual teachers from their personal practice and experience and as being specific to the situations in which it is learned. As a result of this rather narrow view, some think that teachers do not possess a particular form of "know-how" until they can use it with a minimum level of proficiency in their own teaching. The key to this thinking is the belief among many that practical knowledge must be derived from and validated in practice or, to state the point another way, that knowledge does not become practical knowledge until a teacher can do it successfully on a regular basis.

Because practical knowledge tends to be thought of in this narrow way, it is not often thought of as something that can be passed from teacher to teacher. Instead, it is seen as something that individual teachers do but not something they write about or formulate into generally useful statements for other teachers to study. Therefore, it is not considered to be readily codified. The thinking goes somewhat like this: Teachers can pass onto others what they know about teaching but they cannot pass their know-how of teaching (e.g., Eraut, 1994; McNamara & Desforges, 1979; Oakeshott, 1962; Polanyi, 1966, 1969; Ryle, 1949; Tom, 1980).

Contrary to this thinking, however, practical knowledge can be codified into general principles in the same way that other types of professional knowledge can. With this broader view, practical ideas learned by individual teachers can be formulated into principles, explained to and demonstrated for colleagues, tried by them, refined in their own classroom contexts, and developed into widely useful principles of practice—principles available to teachers everywhere.

Tacit Knowledge

Tacit knowledge is often described as the knowledge that people, including teachers, possess without knowing that they know it. It is the knowledge that seems to lie just below a person's level of consciousness. People have it and use it, but cannot explain it to either themselves or others. Sometimes it is equated with intuition, common sense, professional wisdom, "thinking on one's feet," or skilled behavior. It is the kind of knowledge that people know so well that they use it without thinking. Examples include how to ride a bicycle and how to get the attention of a class of students quickly. It is the knowledge that seems to guide successful experienced teachers who have a special, unexplained professional sense of what to do and how to do it.

Some experts on the nature of knowledge suggest that there is an additional aspect of tacit knowledge—a part that teachers store mentally but that never surfaces to the point at which it is recognized and that therefore it is a part of knowledge that is not used. They also suggest that this dormant knowledge could be made useful if elucidated, possibly through significant reflection, self-study, self-analysis, and metacognition (e.g., Dreyfus & Dreyfus, 1986; Eraut, 1994; Polanyi, 1966; Schön, 1983, 1987).

Evidence of the existence of tacit knowledge seems to appear in teacher-to-teacher conversations, such as when a teacher who is observed by a colleague is asked, "I noticed at one point in the lesson you stopped asking the students for more examples and shifted to presenting additional information to them. How did you know it was time to change directions?" In response, the teacher says, "I do not know. It just felt like the right time to do it."

Much of the research of those interested in teacher reflection and metacognition seems devoted to elucidating teacher tacit knowledge and helping teachers come to more thorough and higher levels of understanding of their teaching in general. That research appears to be predicated on the belief that teaching and student learning will improve as teachers understand better what they do, why they do it, and what happens as a result of their doing so. As this happens, the tacit knowledge that becomes visible, understandable, explainable, and talked about can also be placed in the general pool of professional knowledge available to all.

Knowledge in the Context of Use

When teachers select and construct their professional knowledge, whether it comes from the pool of codified knowledge or from professional practice, they do so in terms of how they use that knowledge in their own schools and classrooms—to teach their own students and to accomplish their own goals of student learning (Britzman, 1991; Eraut, 1994). In this context of use, they decide what knowledge is worthy of trial, how that knowledge should be adjusted to fit the local setting, and how it should be applied in practice. Then they try it and determine whether it works. The same is true for competencies and values.

The context of use affects not only how teachers select ideas; it transforms and molds the very nature of the ideas that they select and try. For example, teachers ask themselves how the information they are told in a lecture or the technique they see another teacher demonstrate will fit with their own ways of doing things and work with their own students and in their classrooms. As they listen, they interpret and form that information from the perspective of a potential user—they visualize what they are being told in terms of their own teaching.

This point is made succinctly in the following excerpt from Michael Eraut (1994):

> It is inappropriate to think of knowledge as first being learned then later being used. Learning takes place during use, and the transformation of knowledge into a situationally appropriate form means that it is no longer the same knowledge as it was prior to its first being used. It also follows that learning to use an idea in one context does not guarantee being able to use the same idea in another context: transferring from one context to another requires further learning and the idea itself will be further transformed in the process. (p. 20)

This transformation of information happens because teachers determine the validity and appropriateness of ideas individually and differently from the ways in which that validity and appropriateness are assessed by college teacher educators, researchers, administrators, and policy specialists. Teacher educators and researchers validate their ideas by convincing scholar colleagues that their ideas are worthy of being published; administrators and policy specialists validate their ideas by convincing their various public audiences that their ideas sound good. But teachers—as scholar practitioners—validate their ideas by trying them in their individual classrooms. For teachers, this validation comes in terms of how well they enable their own students to learn (Eraut, 1994, pp. 30-39).

Teacher Validation of Ideas

Because of a teacher's need for validation of ideas through individual performance, the value of any professional knowledge, as far as the teacher is concerned, is determined by its use in helping individual teachers teach rather than by its esoteric origin. The reputation of the developer of a recommended teaching procedure and the sophistication of the research project in which it was developed are less important than the teacher's belief, after trial in his or her classroom, that the procedure helps his or her students learn (Eraut, 1994). If it does not work in this way, it is not likely to be used again because individual teachers hold themselves accountable for their students' learning. They cannot afford to expend their energy and their students' time in ways that do not produce direct results.

Two important aspects of the idea of knowledge in the context of use are important here: (1) teachers understand professional knowledge differently from the way other professional educators understand it, and (2) individual teachers understand professional knowledge differently from each other. This second point can be illustrated as follows. When a number of teachers hear an in-service education presentation about how to handle student classroom misbehavior, different individuals hear different things. For example, preservice teachers who have not yet faced the behavior problems personally, first-year teachers who are anxious about what they might face, teachers who are currently experiencing control problems in the classrooms, teachers who are successful and secure about handling such problems, and teachers who have already tried the specific strategies being presented and are convinced they do not work all hear something different.

Because teachers play such an important role in constructing their professional knowledge in terms of its use, those in learning community schools need to understand the constructed nature of all knowledge, realize the importance of context, and recognize the value of their personal ability to study their own practice and the practice of their school community colleagues. They and their colleagues are the only ones who can develop the professional ideas needed to create the learning they desire for their own students because they are the only scholar practitioners on the scene. They can turn to ideas that have been developed elsewhere as information for their practice but they, and only they, can fit them properly to their use.

This idea that teacher professional knowledge is conceptualized in terms of its use does not contradict the way professional knowledge has been thought of in the past. It only suggests how professional knowledge should be *perceived*. But the suggested change in perception is nonetheless significant because how the knowledge is perceived affects whether it is used and how it is used. Teachers in learning communities recognize this and know that a major part of their professional learning and development occurs every time they reflect on, analyze, and modify their teaching from lesson to lesson, day to day, and year to year. They make their personally developed professional knowledge a major aspect of their teaching and, as a result, are better informed as they make their teaching better.

We realize that this vision of teacher knowledge (and competence and values) is not shared by many current teachers and educators. The more typical perception sees teacher knowledge as being developed by outsiders, delivered to teachers in almost ready-to-be-implemented forms, and applied by teachers in their classrooms without much modification (see Little et al., 1987). This traditional view assumes that ideas, competencies, and values stand on their own— separate from the needs, intentions, and inclinations of the teachers who use them. It assumes that what teachers know, are able to do, and believe is told to them and demonstrated for them and that it is absorbed intact. With this perception, teachers are quickly blamed when ideas delivered to them do not work—the ideas are assumed to be fine and it is the application of them that is assumed to be at fault.

Although we believe this traditional perception of teacher knowledge, competence, and values is wrong, we can think of at least three reasons why it persists. First, constructivist ideas about learning are still not widely understood and rarely applied to an understanding of professional learning. Second, teaching is still usually thought of as a nonintellectual, routine, craftsperson-level replication of the work of experienced masters. Third, the professional learning that emerges from practice and experience is usually not recognized, even by teachers, as knowledge and competence worthy of transmission to other teachers. All three of these points can usually be illustrated by asking almost any group of teachers what new professional information they have learned lately. In response to such a question, teachers typically mention information dispensed to them in workshops and classes conducted by nonteacher outsiders, rather than mentioning something they have discovered personally or with their school colleagues through their own investigation in their own schools or classes. They do this even when they criticize the workshop knowledge they mention as being impractical and not useful.

Parallel to all this is the fact (described in Chapter 2) that teaching is not usually thought of as investigative problem solving or as practice-based experimentation and teachers are not usually thought of as investigative learning professionals. They are seen, instead, as people who do in their work that which others tell them is best practice. Even when teachers do experiment, their experimentation is typically thought of as trial and error that results only in specific information for their own situation rather than as the generation of principles that can be helpful to teachers more broadly. In short, the traditional views of teaching and teacher learning see teacher knowledge, competence, and values as distributed to teachers, instead of created by them.

Professional Knowledge in Learning Communities

For all the reasons discussed throughout this chapter and Chapter 2, we envision teachers in learning community schools constructing professional knowledge (and competence and values) through their entire professional careers. That knowledge does not exist separate from the teachers who construct, possess, and use it or from the settings in which it is constructed and used. Teachers select from professional codified knowledge that which serves their purposes, and they generate their own professional ideas in their work. As they perform professionally, they create ideas that can be powerful enough to be generalized beyond their personal individual use into a form that can

inform other teachers. The flow occurs in two directions. Some knowledge comes initially from multiple outside sources to teachers, who
formulate and develop it as they teach, reflect on it, analyze it, modify
what they do, and incorporate it into their continuing practice. Other
knowledge starts with the teaching of scholar practitioners, who build
their personal insights, expertise, and experimentation into hypotheses
worth testing and then into practice-based theories worthy of dissemi-
nating in abstract form to other practitioners. With this view of professional knowledge, teachers are seen as continuously learning experts
intellectually responsible for their own professional development.

In essence, the professional learning of teachers can be described
as follows: Beginning teacher education students bring with them to
their professional study all their previously learned ideas, competencies, and value perspectives. In their preservice study and the induction years of their learning to teach, they formulate additional general
principles about learning, students, teaching, and schools from their
own background; from codified knowledge, skills, and values; and
from ideas gathered while visiting real teaching situations and schools.
At that point they are judged ready to begin the practice of teaching.
Then they practice the profession of teaching by combining their previous learning, the codified knowledge, the observation-based information, and the practical knowledge they develop along the way to
apply it to specific instructional situations, classes, and schools in their
own day-to-day teaching. With each lesson they teach and each
schoolwide activity they participate in, they adjust, update, and up-
grade what they know, do, and believe. As they do this, they consistently learn more, but in addition, they perfect their ability to study
their own learning metacognitively—they get better at teaching while
they also get better at studying teaching. The dual processes of teaching and getting better at teaching continue in spiral fashion as teacher
scholar practitioners build ever increasingly and ever more substan-
tively their own knowledge, competence, and values about learning
and teaching. The first few years probably produce their most noticeable professional learning, but the learning never stops; the knowledge, competence, and values continue to develop.

Implications for Teacher Education

When teacher professional knowledge and learning are
thought of in these ways, one can see that teacher education also

needs to be reconceptualized. Instead of it being the delivery of ideas, competencies, and values to teachers, it needs to be thought of as the helping of teachers to educate the students they are pledged to serve. To the extent that teaching is professional practice—investigative problem identification and problem solving—teacher educators need to be co-problem solvers and coinvestigators. To the extent that professional learning is a matter of intellectual construction, teacher educators need to be coconstructors and colearners. To the extent that schools are learning communities, teacher educators need to be professional participants—committed fully to serving the schools' mission.

CHAPTER FOUR

Getting There From Here

*What might the journey toward ideal
learning community schools look like?*

If the learning community schools that we envision are to become
realities, all of us associated with schools, student learning, and
teaching need to change our professional thinking and the ways in
which we act on that thinking. Better ways of implementing old ideas
and minor changes in those old ideas are simply not enough. We need
to replace those ideas and the intellectual principles that underlie
what we now do and then act in terms of these different principles and
their accompanying assumptions. In our view, the shifts in thinking
and acting need to occur in three overlapping phases.

First, we need to formulate clear forward-directed images of what
we believe learning community schools will look like when they are
developed in local settings—as local applications of the images of
schools, learning, teaching, and teacher learning described in Chapters 2 and 3—and we need to use these images to guide all our getting-
better action. To do this, we need to rethink the purpose of our
schools, how the schools function, how learning takes place, what
teachers and students do, who decides what they do, and how teachers learn. Neither the new thinking nor the changes that follow will be
easy; neither can they be superficial. They will involve uncomfortable
cultural and intellectual struggles for everyone—new metaphors,
assumptions, and belief systems; new priorities and practices; new
explanations for what we do and new justifications for doing so; and
new bases for determining if and how well we are succeeding.

Second, we need to look seriously and honestly at what we now
have and are now doing and validly assess in terms of our new images

what and why we have and do them. We need to determine the strengths and weaknesses of how we formulate and articulate our mission, organize our schools, create student learning, conduct teaching, and improve our professional work. To do this, we need to revisit our thinking about our schools' missions, purposes, and goals; re-evaluate ourselves, our professional colleagues, our school cultures and climates, and our professional motives in light of those modified views; and align them with our vision of learning community schools in the distance. We need to hold high the ideals we envision for learning community schools and probe deeply and intrusively as we measure ourselves and all around us against these ideals. We need to admit that we are not as good at what we do or as successful as we would like to be—that we are still learning and will always be learning—and we must not be defensive about admitting our imperfections. We must also realize that as times change, even good ideas and practices become dated and less appropriate.

Third, we need to journey expeditiously and persistently from where we are now toward where we want to be—toward that ideal vision of learning community schools in the distance. To do this, we need to look hard at each school activity and decision and ask, How does this build a stronger learning community, encourage constructivist student learning, enhance investigative, problem identification, and problem-solving teaching, and stimulate practice-based teacher learning—how does it teach students well now and how will it teach them better in the future? Then we need to ask, How can we improve on what we have? Where are the points of intrusion into our current practice? How can we convert these points of intrusion into places of departure? How can we develop vehicles for change that will move us from these points to where we want to go? Answers to these how-can-we-improve questions become our hypotheses for trying something different, assessing its effects, and moving forward—always learning, always improving.

The journeys cannot be tightly preplanned and managed by strategic-planner-type leaders; they must follow less clear courses akin to those described by chaos theorists—many things happening at the same time, some planned, some not; all affecting each other, sometimes mutually supportive, sometimes clashing—moving toward the same general direction but not on consistently parallel paths. In Michael Fullan's (1993) words, these journeys need to be journeys "of uncertainty," journeys that pursue visions but are not "blinded by them" (p. 40). No one overall leader is in charge, but people strive together so they make their individual choices and motives mesh. Different people have their own views of what is happening, why it is happening, and if they like what they see, but they persist at doing their part better in spite of their differences. They are team players as well as individual professional experts. Progress is not judged on the bases of consistency and compatibility across the many parts and individual tasks, but on the direction and extent of the general movement toward the images of the ideal on the horizon (see Fullan, 1993, 1997).

In the next part of this chapter, we describe ways in which we believe we can move toward the ideal learning community school we envision—ways in which we can proceed through the three phases of change just outlined. We describe in some detail each of the following:

- Using the images of what our schools should be like as guides
- Recognizing the difficulty of the task of change
- Recognizing the importance of a positive attitude toward change
- Assessing our current schools and school practices in terms of the images we have in mind
- Journeying from the present toward the ideal

Then we describe several efforts at school change that can serve as examples of points of intrusion, places of departure, and vehicles for change for journeys toward learning community schools—efforts that have been or are now being taken that we think are worthy of closer study.

Pursuing Images

The images we have of our schools define what the schools actually are. They provide their justification and the intellectual bases on which they are created and sustained; they guide how schools develop and evolve over time. They frame how school cultures, student learning, teaching, and teacher learning are understood and what each of these dimensions of schooling is expected to be like in the future. They supply mental pictures of schools, how they function and should function, what they accomplish and should accomplish, and how they are and should be measured. For example, schools thought of as factories and teaching viewed as the delivery of teacher-held information to student minds are expected to "produce" informed students whose learning is assessed by how much information they have absorbed. Also, teachers who judge success in student learning in the form of high SAT scores believe they get better at teaching when their instruction produces higher test results, and those who use managing student classroom behavior as a primary professional task interpret success in terms of well-behaved classes. In similar fashion, teacher educators and supervisors who think of teacher education as deficit reduction tell teachers what they are doing wrong, how they should be teaching, and then watch to see if they do what they have been told (e.g., Little, 1993).

The images that people hold of schools and what happens in them—what they are and what they should be—develop in an evolving way over time. They are derived from values broader than those associated with schools and schooling alone—beliefs about society, people in general, the nature of learning, and the role of schools in relation to all these. The images grow from what people know about schools—from their own personal experience as well as from their more general knowledge—and they are influenced by what they expect of school and society as well as what they hope for them.

Therefore, those of us who want to create schools significantly different from those typical of today need to focus first on images—on the ways in which people at large, as well as professional educators, think of schools, student learning, teaching, and teacher learning—and we need to replace these images with ones more forward directed. In short, we need new thinking, thinking that will create new metaphors. We need to build in people's minds what some educational writers call new *mindscapes* of schools, learning, and teaching, and these new mindscapes need to envision schools in the distance, on the horizon—schools the way they could be if all conditions were as we would like (Sergiovanni, 1996). Then we need to use these mindscapes as destinations that describe what is expected of our local schools—the culture in which these schools operate, the ways they function, how students learn, how teachers teach, how decisions are made, and how everything is judged. We need to use the new images to establish, support, guide, and sanction new ways of doing things.

A Difficult Journey

Of course, changes of this type—replacing old mindscapes with new ones, substituting new metaphors for old ones, and thinking more probingly about school images—are not easy to make. They are difficult for a number of reasons (Fullan, 1991, 1992a, 1992b, 1992c, 1993, 1994a, 1994b, 1995, 1996a, 1996b, 1997; Myers, 1995b, 1996a, 1996b, 1997a; Sarason, 1990, 1995, 1996, 1997).

Changing Our Thinking

These changes are difficult because of the very fact that they are changes in the way we think rather than changes in how we act. They challenge the ways in which we see things—often ways that have remained in place and been unchallenged for a long time. They question assumptions that underlie what is expected and beliefs about how things should be. They are deeper than shifts in how things are done. School operations and teaching practices can be seen, but the ideas that guide these activities are more nebulous. Different people, even those who work together, have different perspectives of what individual ideas mean and how they should be transformed into action. So we are uneasy when we are asked to change the ways in which we think about things. We want assurances that the new ideas are definitely better than the old and we want clear senses of what to expect if we accept the new. But ideas by themselves cannot provide this security.

Using New Lenses

A second reason why changing images is difficult has to do with the nature of change. As Peter Senge (1990) describes in *The Fifth Discipline,* at the early stages of modifying the ways we look at things, we are imprisoned by our old thinking. No matter how hard we try to see things through new lenses, we continue, in varying degrees, to interpret new ideas in old ways—through intellectual perspectives in our heads at the time—and these old ideas in our heads are derived from past experiences and old ways of thinking. So we typically place our new ideas, at least partially, in the old categories of mind that have guided our thinking in the past. And we act accordingly. For example, administrators who become convinced that site-based management is worthy of pursuing often decide personally and individually that their schools will "do it." Then they draft directives announcing the decision, explaining how it will be implemented, and describing top-down plans for assessing its success against external criteria. Teachers in this situation frequently accept the fact that they have been told that they will start making many of their own professional decisions and wait for more specific directions on how, how much, and what they will decide. In this scenario, procedures might change and more meetings might be called, but the old decision makers tend to continue the decision making and the decisions tend to produce the same results.

Confronting Old Structures and Old Ways

Third,[3] when images are pursued, they are pursued within the structures and by the mechanism in place at the time. There is not enough time and not enough information available to shift structures and mechanisms immediately. These in-place structures and mechanisms evolved from old thinking and old ways of doing things. They are usually more suited to the old than the new and, as a result, do not serve the implementation process very well. As a result, those thinking ahead about what will happen as they pursue the new images are often slowed by realistic concerns about how their ideas will actually be implemented. For instance, when school faculty begin to teach reading from multiple authentic sources instead of from a basal reading series, someone has to order, gather, and pay for those materials. Old-style textbook adoption committees and a single order form sent to one supplier will no longer do the job. More and different patterns of bureaucratic work are required and bureaucrats and bureaucracies change slowly. If the process takes too long or is too troublesome—if the correct books do not arrive when the teachers need them—those who liked the ideas at first will start to question if the effort is worth the burden.

Converting Others

Fourth,[4] when school professionals change their thinking, the ideas of other influential people are also challenged and, therefore, those other people need to be converted to the new thinking or at least convinced enough to acquiesce. In fact, some experts on education reform attribute much failure of reform to the inability of reformers to attract all school stakeholders to their cause. School board members, parents, politicians, voters, and chamber of commerce leaders, for example, need to accept the new ideas even though their knowledge of schools is limited and their perspectives are just as dated and narrow as those of anyone else. Before they agree to a change in thinking, they usually want to be assured that the change is a correct one, and they often want that assurance before a plan is implemented and evidence is generated. At a minimum, they want quick, clear, irrefutable results that support the new ideas. Of course, ideas by their very nature are too abstract and vague to provide such assurance.

Making the Change Fit

Fifth, images have to come from somewhere and often the places and circumstances where they were developed and flourished and from which they are drawn, such as business settings or schools that operate in different environments, are not the same as the schools into which they are imported. This fact seems to be overlooked frequently by education reformers and school restructurers who use adopt-a-model or adopt-a-package approaches to school improvement. The fact that models—such as management by objectives, total quality management, any number of curriculum packages, or a particular style of teaching—work in some locales is no assurance that they will work somewhere else. If a set of practices works well in one setting, it is because it is supported by many compatible assumptions and beliefs; if similar assumptions and beliefs are not present to undergird the practice in a new location, the anticipated results and meaningful changes are not likely to occur.[5] New images of schools and schooling must be compatible with and fitted to the circumstances in which they are being applied.

Because of all these difficulties in pursuing serious thought-based change—change in ideas as well as in action—the images of what we want our learning community schools to be like when our efforts succeed gives us not only a sense of direction but also a view of what is ahead and a sustaining force that keeps us moving toward our goal. The images describe both where we are going and where we want to be. Although everyone in the learning community school does not have to have a personal, emotional attachment to every aspect of each image, they as a whole do need to desire enough of the vision to commit their time and energy to the tasks of making the vision real (Myers, 1997b).

 ## Attitude, Attitude, Attitude

The desire to change—to move toward the images in the distance—is not typically present across all the professionals in schools today. On the contrary, most school people find comfort in doing things as they have been doing them in the past as long as the results are what they expect. So they tend to accept change only when something no longer works. This is understandable, of course, because doing things differently involves risk, insecurity, and usually more work. Therefore, those of us who wish to move toward new visions of learning community schools must develop a special willingness to push ahead from the familiar and secure to the less well known—possibly the virtually unknown—and to that which is risky and maybe threatening. That willingness to move ahead involves a complicated collection of attitudes, characteristics, and traits—those that can be possessed not only by individuals but also by groups, organizations, and communities as a whole.

Cultivating such a willing attitude toward change is part of the getting-there-from-here effort. The attitude cannot be expected to be present in a persuasive way at the start; it must be developed along the way and it must be central to the learning community atmosphere.

What constitutes such an attitude and how can it be cultivated, enhanced, and sustained? We think this willingness to change consists of many overlapping and multifaceted personality and character elements that individuals and communities possess in varying degrees. We think it is more affective—deals primarily with feelings and emotions—than cognitive; it develops more through nurturing than manipulation; and it can be spread best through education, good will, and the inviting of others to join a caring, sharing, and winning cause. We think it includes characteristics such as

- Freedom of thought
- Inquisitiveness
- Hunger for meaning

- Desire to experiment
- Willingness to take risks
- Courage to fail
- Flexibility
- Adaptability
- Self-knowledge
- Confidence
- Controlled individualism
- Commitment to ideals
- Passion for success
- Empathy for colleagues (see Gardner, 1981)

All individuals and groups that set out on journeys toward learning community schools should possess a smattering of these characteristics—the more the better. But it is unrealistic to anticipate that all will possess most of them or that such traits happen spontaneously in people. On the other hand, these characteristics can be developed and nurtured and they can be passed from individual to individual and group to group. They can infiltrate a developing school community to the extent that they become part of the learning culture itself—they can become the identifying characteristics of the culture and the individuals who make up the community.

Although we do not attach specialized meanings to most of these terms as we use them here, we explain several of them briefly below to illustrate further their importance. (In doing so, we draw heavily on the writings of Gardner, 1981.)

- Freedom of thought—openness to speculate, explore, inquire, imagine, consider, formulate, create continuously in a manner that is unrestrained from within or without (Garner, 1981, p. 74).
- Inquisitiveness—a strong-felt desire to pursue freedom of thought.
- Hunger for meaning—an insatiable desire to figure things out, to organize what we know into coherent patterns, to make things meaningful, to know how things fit with each other and when we ourselves fit in that scheme of things; to seek truth (Gardner, 1981, pp. 100-104; Kierkegaard, 1935 in Bretall, 1946, pp. 4-5; Tillich, 1952).

- Willingness to take risks—an inclination to take a chance, to explore the unknown, to counter a fear of failure, to try again in spite of previous failure, to do what others shy away from trying, to move ahead of others on one's own (Gardner, 1981, pp. 14-15).

- Flexibility—to change directions, to shift strategies; to "play with" an idea for a while, to test its utility, to look at it from different angles; to approach a situation, issue, or problem from different perspectives; to maintain a degree of detachment from conventional categories and obstructions and from one's own past ideas, attitudes, and habits of mind; to tolerate ambiguity, internal conflict, and discomfort as one works toward a goal (Gardner, 1981, pp. 37-38).

- Self-knowledge—to know one's self-strengths, weaknesses, emotions, proclivities, anxieties, likes, dislikes, vulnerabilities, inclinations, potential sources of embarrassment, and so on; to grasp what makes one what he or she is and how he or she fits with the environment in which he or she lives (Erikson, 1956; Gardner, 1981, pp. 12-14).

- Controlled individualism—individual autonomy regulated by a personal sense of moral responsibility; a personal freedom to do and act but within the confines of a broader social good; a balancing of individual freedoms with social commitments (Gardner, 1981, pp. 86-95).

John Gardner (1981) expresses how important attitude is for tasks such as creating learning community schools in the following, about more general social and individual renewal:

Individuals cannot achieve renewal if they do not believe in the possibility of it. Nor can a society. At all times in history there have been individuals and societies whose attitudes toward the future have been such as to thwart, or at least greatly impede, the processes of renewal.

There is a readily discernible difference between the society (or individual) that is oriented to the future and the one that is oriented to the past. Some individuals and societies look forward and have the future ever in mind, others are preoccupied with the past and are antiquarian in their interests. The former have a vivid sense of what they are becoming, the latter a vivid sense of what they have been. The former are fascinated by the novelty of each day's experience, the latter have a sense of having seen everything.

No society is likely to renew itself unless its dominant orientation is to the future. This is not to say that a society can ignore its past. A people without historians would be as crippled as an individual with amnesia. They would not know who they were. In helping a society to achieve self-knowledge, the historian serves the cause of renewal. But in the renewing society the historian consults the past in the service of the present and the future.

The society capable of continuous renewal not only is oriented toward the future but looks ahead with some confidence. This is not to say that blind optimism prevails; it is simply to say that hopelessness does not make for renewal. . . .

In a society capable of renewal, people not only welcome the future and the changes it brings but believe they can have a hand in shaping that future. (pp. 105-107)

 ## Assessing Current School Conditions and Practices

As we develop our images of each of the four dimensions of our ideal learning community schools, we also need to assess where our current school, its practices, and its participants stand in terms of these images—How do they match up?—and we need to conduct the assessing honestly and thoroughly. For example, we need to ask general questions such as, To what extent and in what ways is our school a culture and a community? What do we do to enhance a community ethos of the school? What do we do that moves us away from it? Do we subscribe to a central mission of quality learning for all? What do we do that shows this? Do we see students as constructivist, experiential learners? In what ways do our actions reflect and contradict this view? Do we think of teaching as investigative problem identification and problem solving? Which schoolwide and teacher-specific approaches to teaching are consistent with our image and which are not? Are our professional development activities educative, constructivist, and student-centered rather than deficit-reduction in their orientation?

As we raise these questions, we must acknowledge that doing so requires major commitments of energy and time. It is not something that can be done outside of school time or in periodic, noncontiguous, in-service education activities. It has to be built into the work that all school professionals expect to do as a core component of their normal responsibilities. It has to be serious self-study.

Self-Study Through Honest Inquiry

The questions asked need to be probing and raised in ways that provoke serious thought. They need to prompt investigative self-study—thorough inquiry into what is happening in all aspects of the school, why it is happening, and if it should be happening. All answers need to be compared with the idealized images of what the questioners hope the school will become. When asked and answered appropriately, the questions and their answers will identify foci for both immediate and future action—things to work on—as the journey toward the envisioned learning community school begins and proceeds.

As we ask and answer the questions, we need to remember their purpose. The questions are not for summative evaluation—to determine if the school or one of its components and its people are good enough. They are not part of a comparison with other schools, teachers, and students. They are not to produce data for parents, the local newspaper, or the chamber of commerce. The questions and the questioning are intended to stimulate analyses that compare what is with our own images of what should be,—to define the starting point for change and set direction. An early step in any journey involves figuring out where one is at the beginning.

As we think of the numerous efforts to change schools that we have observed, participated in, and read about, we realize that there is a great danger that questions such as these will not be addressed appropriately and adequately in most school settings—that they will be avoided, taken lightly, treated superficially, or responded to dishonestly. In fact, many of those who study current school improvement endeavors see the lack of sincere self-study as a major reason why schools do not get better. Often, posturing substitutes for analysis, and public relations has priority over improving practice—sounding good attracts greater interest than being good.

This is not surprising, of course. Honestly raised, targeted, probing questions threaten schools, their activities, and their participants. They attack false facades, expose posturing, reject rationalizing, challenge assumptions, question beliefs, identify weaknesses, threaten egos, and generally scare everyone. They open all to criticism and show that even those who are good could be better. But on the other hand, honestly pursued, investigative self-study questions tell us not only where we are but also how we can get better and what to improve.

Raising and answering investigative, self-study-type questions in terms of our images of what our schools should be produces three important results central to creating learning community schools.

- They identify where things stand at the start of the process.
- They set directions for improvement—for movement toward the ideal.
- They focus school participants' thinking on the task of aligning mission, purpose, goals, and images of what should be with day-to-day school conditions, structures, activities, and individual actions.

They ask, Where and what are we? In which direction should we be moving? How does what we believe and expect of ourselves match with what we do?

Initial Questions

For an investigative self-study process to produce the kinds of insights and suggestions that can be used to move schools toward our learning community ideal, it needs to raise initial questions that possess two somewhat contrasting orientations. First, the questions need to be relevant to and connected with the school's current circumstances and conditions; second, they need to incorporate the images of the ideal school community on the horizon. Without the first orientation, the self-study will not be fair or accurate; without the second, it will not be future-directed—in either case, the findings and motivation expected from the self-study will not be very useful for the getting-better task they are expected to serve.

We suggest, therefore, that the guiding questions of school self-studies be organized around the dimensions of schooling that we have used to describe our four views of learning community schools—each set focusing on key characteristics within each dimension. Our suggested questions appear below in four sections. Each section begins with a few general questions and more specific questions follow. Often, we raise the questions in both positive and negative terms and we do so purposely—we think doing this makes the questions more probing and more stimulating of serious reflection; it also seems to help counter defensiveness.

Questions concerning the school as a morally based community of learners

General Questions

In what ways and to what extent is our school a cultural community of learners? In what ways is it not a community or not a culture?

Response:

In what ways do we think of our school as doing morally good work? In what ways does it fall short?

Response:

How strongly and in what ways does our school pursue the mission of learning for all? In what ways could the mission be extended to include more students and other community members?

Response:

What evidence is there that our community feels a unity to which we all subscribe and in which we all share? What activities and feelings contradict that sense of unity?

Response:

How do the ways in which we look at teachers (including ourselves) and at what teachers do in the community reflect beliefs that teachers are the predominant professional experts and leading decision-makers in the community? Which actions clash with such beliefs?

Response:

What evidence of optimism exists in our school? Where is it lacking or why is it weak?

Response:

More Specific Questions

What evidence do we have that a moral mission to which all subscribe exists in our school?

Response:

If all professionals in our school were asked to write individual statements that describe our school's mission, what would those statements include?

Response:

What are the values, beliefs, rituals, traditions, norms, and loyalties that people of our school share in common?

Response:

In what ways do we feel that we belong? What evidence do we have that we are wanted?

Response:

What do we do to show that we care about and for each other? How do others show this for us?

Response:

In what ways do we assume schoolwide responsibilities as well as the specific responsibilities not normally expected of us? When and why do we renege?

Response:

What evidence is there that community goals supersede individual and personal ones? When is the reverse true?

Response:

When community decisions need to be made, to what extent and in what ways do teachers make them? When are teachers told rather than asked? By whom?

Response:

How do nonteacher community participants respond to teacher needs and professional requests?

Response:

In what ways do the functions of teaching and learning in our school prescribe the procedures and structures of the school? When and in what ways do procedures and structures determine what and how teaching and learning take place?

Response:

Do we often say, "They won't let us. . . ."? If so, why do we say this and who are "they"?

Response:

Questions concerning learning as
experience-based intellectual construction

General Questions

To what extent and in what ways does the work students do and what we expect of them reflect an experience-based, constructivist perspective of learning? In what ways do we contradict that perspective?

Response:

How do the number and kind of active learning experiences that we provide for our students compare with more passive experiences?

Response:

In what ways are all individuals in the school community learners every day?

Response:

Which members of our school community enjoy their learning experiences? Which do not? What makes the difference?

Response:

More Specific Questions

Do we create experiences for students as often, or more often, than tell them information we want them to know?

Response:

Are we as focused on what happens in students as much or more than on what we do to them?

Response:

How do we encourage students to solve problems and construct their own meaning? In what ways do we stifle either or both?

Response:

Do we think student learning experiences are more important than achievement results? What do we do that shows this? What do we do that suggests the opposite?

Response:

Do we use student assessments as measures of learning in progress as much as we use them as indicators of success?

Response:

Do we, as teachers, coach students regularly? In what ways do we do this?

Response:

What evidence do we have that illustrates that teacher learning is a dominant school goal?

Response:

In what ways do our administrators, supervisors, and other support staff learn from their work? How do they get better because of what they do?

Response:

Questions concerning teaching as career-long, investigative problem identification and problem solving

General Questions

To what extent and in what ways do we think of teaching as the professional practice of knowledgeable and skilled experts? What evidence is there that this is not our thinking?

Response:

To what extent do we teachers see ourselves as constructivist learners who get better because of what we learn as we teach?

Response:

What evidence is there that we teachers see ourselves, and are seen by others, as investigative problem identifiers and problem solvers—scholar practitioners? What evidence is there that we are seen as only craftspersons who perform routine tasks?

Response:

In what ways do we analyze our own, and our colleagues', practice? What indicators are there that we repeat the same teaching practices year after year with little change?

Response:

In what ways does our school atmosphere reflect a professional culture of inquiry?

Response:

More Specific Questions

What evidence is there that teaching is our central professional school activity?

Response:

In what ways do we teachers study student learning and our own teaching practices, and base our subsequent teaching on what we learn?

Response:

How do we develop our own theories in our practice of teaching? What ideas have we developed lately?

Response:

In what ways do we share professional ideas and practices with our colleagues?

Response:

What evidence do we have that our teaching is learner centered? What indications are there that it is not?

Response:

How often do we admit that we do not know the appropriate way to teach particular students in specific situations? Are we embarrassed when we do? Do others help us find out?

Response:

What evidence is there that we approach our teaching as an intellectual endeavor?

Response:

In what ways do we and our colleague teachers address teaching situations collaboratively? When and how often do we struggle with our teaching problems and frustrations in isolation?

Response:

Do we expect to get better as we teach? Are we succeeding at this? How do we know?

Response:

Do we think of our teaching as experimentation? In what ways? When we do, how do we assess the results?

Response:

Do we help our colleagues learn? Do they help us?

Response:

Questions concerning professional knowledge, competence, and value perspectives as developed in practice

General Questions

To what extent and in what ways do we develop our own ideas about our best practice and how do we test these ideas in our classes?

Response:

How do we learn about research and scholarly ideas and how do we use these ideas in our teaching? How do we determine if they work for us?

Response:

In what ways do we analyze our technical knowledge about teaching and formulate it into principles of practice that we can explain to colleagues? How frequently do we do this?

Response:

How do we probe the tacit knowledge that we possess about our teaching? When we do, how do we use the ideas we discover?

Response:

To what extent and in what ways do all professionals in our school learn from each other? How are we a community of professional learners?

Response:

More Specific Questions

To what extent and in what ways do we learn new ideas about teaching during each year that we teach?

Response:

Where do we turn for new ideas about how to teach and how to conduct a school? Why do we do so?

Response:

How do we decide which new ideas about teaching are good for us and our students?

Response:

What new ideas have we learned lately about the subject matter content we teach? About how to teach it better or more appropriately?

Response:

How do we fit together pedagogical knowledge and subject-matter content knowledge so the two dimensions of knowledge make sense for us?

Response:

What new ideas have we learned lately about good ways to teach?

Response:

In what ways do we add each year to our personal pool of technical knowledge?

Response:

_____

To what extent and in what ways do we explore and analyze what we do automatically as we teach? Why do we do this in these ways?

Response:

_____

In what ways do we change ideas we have learned about teaching so they fit our school, classes, students, and personal teaching style?

Response:

_____

To what extent and in what ways do we teach and learn from our teacher colleagues?

Response:

_____

Although questions such as these will not by themselves transform schools into learning communities, if they are used to stimulate serious, forward-directed, positive thinking—as different from blaming or self-congratulating posturing—they are means on which to begin an honest professional assessment of where a school is in terms of a learning community vision. They can prompt and guide serious inquiry that will produce both analyses of current conditions and direction for what to do next to move a school and the learning and teaching that occur within it closer to the ideal. The questions, in short, serve three purposes: (1) they help us figure out where we are and how we do things at present; (2) they frame the getting-better task before us in terms of the ideal on the horizon—the target for the task; and (3) they suggest some of the areas on which we need to work, as well as the ones we might chose to tackle first.

 ## The Nature of the Journeys

As we educators move from our present ideas, school situations, and ways of conducting our professional work toward learning community schools, we need to acknowledge and keep clearly in our minds three critical points:

1. The changes we are pursuing are conceptual and cultural—they are changes in thinking and in belief systems, not just changes in how we do things.

2. Our journeys toward the ideal learning community are different from the ideal communities we seek—the journeys have to do with paths and means of movement along these paths; the visions of the learning communities are desired, hypothetical destinations.

3. Each school's journey is unique to that school community.

This means that the changes involved in our journeys are not simple matters of throwing out the old and substituting the new as if the process were as easy as moving from one teaching job to another or from an old school building to a newer one. We have to evolve and adjust in some form of progression from present ways of seeing, understanding, and believing things to new assumptions and different habits of mind. Gradual shifts and adjustments must occur all along the way; all the while, we must continue to teach our students and operate our schools and classrooms as best we can—even as our ideas of what is best are shifting (Myers, 1996b, 1997b).

An Evolution Toward New Rules

As we have already suggested, the journeys as a whole are not merely matters of gradual reform, step-by-step restructuring, or partnership formation. Although they involve evolution, evolution is not their purpose. Their purpose is to replace the schools we now have with new school cultures—in which learning is experienced and enjoyed by everyone and where everyone fits, belongs, and bonds. The process is evolutionary, the anticipated changes as a whole are revolutionary.

To the extent that the journeys succeed, each of the following dichotomies that now pervade school thinking and guide educators' daily action will fade from view: teaching and learning, teacher and learner, theory and practice, research and implementation, teacher educator and teacher, preservice teacher preparation and in-service continuing teacher education, novice and expert, and leader and follower. Each of these dichotomies represents a thinking about schools that separates instead of unifies, and learning communities, by their very nature, unify rather than separate—they focus all community members, elements, and processes on a single moral mission: learning.

Therefore, the journey of each school toward its envisioned learning community replacement should be described, understood, and tracked in terms of the evolution of roles and emphases within roles that will occur for each school participant. The new and more emphasized roles that should be anticipated include the following.

- *Roles for teachers*—inquirer, investigator, problem identifier, problem solver, creator of student learning experiences, constructivist developer of professional knowledge, professional learner, collaborative professional colleague, analytical learner, researcher, scholar practitioner, professional decision maker, center of professional authority and power, and community leader

- *Roles for principals, supervisors, and other administrators*—professional learner, respondent to teacher needs, coach, supporter of teacher initiatives, follower (as well as leader), securer of resources, source of psychological support, cultivator of inquiry and experimentation, provider of security, supplier of recognition and praise, guide toward better practice, discriminating professional evaluator, terminator of incompetent performers, and maintainer of a desirable school climate

- *Roles for educational policymakers*—supporter of the school mission, protector of professional privilege, cheerleader, supplier of resources, stimulator of recognition, employer of teacher experts, professional learner, fully participating community member, and advocate
- *Roles for student*—fully engaged community participant, active learner, intellectual explorer and experimenter, leader (as well as follower), and primary focus of all community activity
- *Roles of parent*—community participant, resource and supporter of students and teachers, learner, teacher, securer of needed resources, communicator with broader community, and advocate

In similar fashion, all others in the broader community that surrounds and supports the school should be seen as different, with more integral roles than the ones they possess at the start of the journey.

These journeys toward learning community schools are not orchestrated, single-file marches toward one clear point in the future. Although there are visions on the horizon and each vision should include the four dimensions we have described, those visions look different to each observer and many of their specific characteristics are unclear to all. They are made up of many parts, efforts, and individual tasks.

The journeys also involve travelers of all types, at all levels of the educative enterprise—teachers, administrators, students, parents— each toiling in his or her own professional space; each with his or her own ideas, dreams, and sense of direction; each trying to get better at what he or she does; each helping others in the task; and each pursuing the same general ideal in his or her own way. All are moving at once, at different paces, on different levels, with different styles; but all go in the same general direction when the direction is broadly conceived. All want to improve the learning and professional culture of their school, but they have to invent that culture as they go.

In a way, these journeys, when they are succeeding and moving forward, remind us of a comment attributed to a former major league baseball player who was said to have described his and his colleagues' professional work as follows: Baseball is a team sport, but nine individuals committed to and constantly striving as hard as they can to achieve their personal goals make a great team. The journeys are team efforts in which all community participants establish and achieve their personal goals in terms of their visions of what their community can be. Each has his and her role and personal way of fulfilling it, but everyone strives for the common good.

Who Leads and What Do They Do?

To a great extent, the presumption that journeys toward learning community schools need leaders—and by implication followers of those leaders—exemplifies the kind of thinking that learning community cultures seek to replace. In ideal learning communities, everyone does his or her part, roles evolve, tasks are unique to situations: Some people lead and follow at the same time, some lead more often than others, some follow most of the time; and some lead at big efforts and others lead at small ones. Who does what gets all mixed up and everyone joins in. This is how it should be as the journeys approach the ideal community (Barth, 1990; Fullan, 1992a, 1992b, 1992c, 1993, 1994a, 1994b, 1995, 1996a, 1996b, 1997; Lambert et al., 1995, 1997; Myers, 1996b, 1997b; Sarason, 1996, 1997).

But, as we suggested earlier, each school has to start its journey from where it happens to be at the time—and that point is usually far from the ideal. The school must continue to teach students and use the talents and perspectives of the professionals already on the scene. This usually means that those who lead initially tend to be those who are already leading at the time.

If the journeys are to make noticeable progress, however, what those leaders do and how they interact with other school community participants must change in several ways. First, the leaders of the journeys must lead two efforts simultaneously, not one: (1) the journey toward the ideal—the change effort; and (2) the current, evolving school effort as it serves its students. The two efforts cannot be blended into one. In fact, a major goal of the change effort is to reduce the current leaders' old-style power and decision-making authority—to cultivate a leadership among all community professionals that replaces that previously conducted in top-down fashion.

Second, these leaders of the journeys must share their leadership. They must *build community,* not *authorize* and *direct* action, as would be appropriate in an old-style technical, rational, business-type school organization. They need to promote community identification, loyalty, cooperation, a sense of moral goodness and mission, and the other elements of a morally based cultural community that we described in Chapter 2. As they do, they must allow their more traditional leadership status to dissipate.

To illustrate this shift in leadership, we turn to a characterization of motivation that has been discussed for a number of years by organizational behavior theorists (Hachman et al., 1975; Herzberg et al., 1959; Senge, 1990). The idea can be explained in terms of three guiding principles that can be capsulated as follows:

- What gets rewarded gets done.
- What is rewarding gets done.
- What is good gets done. (For an explanation of these ideas in summary form, see Sergiovanni, 1992, pp. 57-66)

Old-style school leaders, those who still follow business-based, technical-rational organizational models, tend to subscribe to the first of these principles, and therefore they see their primary role as providers and withholders of rewards. They place themselves above teachers and entice them to be good educators of students by rewarding them for doing so—the school leaders decide what is good and issue positive or negative behavioral stimuli.

In contrast, those working at becoming learning-community-style leaders focus increasingly on the second and third principles as the bases for their leadership. They see that rewards for all—including teachers—in learning communities are intrinsic, not extrinsic and manipulated. Instead of giving or withholding artificial rewards, they recognize that rewards for a learning community rest in the morally good work that is being done—in the mission that is being pursued. More specifically, they lead (1) by helping all in the community to recognize the inherent goodness and rewarding nature of teaching, and (2) by assuring that everyone experiences the success, recognition, and satisfaction due them. They help teachers become more knowledgeable, more satisfied, and more intrinsically rewarded for their work, which, according to research by Mihalyi Csikszentmihalyi (1990), happens when competent teachers are so involved in their teaching that the burdens and difficulties associated with their tasks do not matter enough to dissuade them—when they enjoy their work so much that they will do it at great cost for the sheer sake of doing it (p. 4).

Third, the leaders of the journeys must keep reminding the others of the vision toward which they are moving and keep encouraging them to stay the course. How they do this—the leadership styles that they use—here again must evolve toward that of the community leader encompassed in the vision. Educative, supportive, coaching, mediating, cheerleading, counseling, and caring roles must increasingly come to the fore.

Fourth, the leaders of the journey must gradually come to see themselves as individuals on a team instead of leaders of the pack. They must play their roles while others do the same. Eventually, everyone will do the part that each does best and prefers to do, and everyone will be responsible for the team's successes and failures; in the face of failures, everyone will reassess, learn from the mistakes, and make the necessary corrections—that is what learning communities do.

Intrusions, Departures, and Vehicles for Change

In Chapter 1, we suggest that journeys toward ideal learning community schools can begin by (1) identifying points of intrusion into the normal life of each of our schools, (2) making these points of intrusion into places of departure for the journey, and (3) constructing at those places of departure vehicles for change that will carry us toward the horizon. Now we offer suggestions of what some of these intrusion points, departures, and vehicles might be. All the suggestions come in the form of examples—not exemplars or models—and the examples are of three types. First, we describe rather small initial efforts that can be started and developed by a few building-level colleagues with a minimum of outside support or direction. Second, we offer a possible schoolwide experiment for your consideration. Third, we describe a select number of large-scale reform endeavors that have been generating significant activity and getting good reviews nationally. Before we proceed, however, we want to repeat our caution: We offer none of these as either existing learning community models to be adopted or recommended ways to create learning community schools. We offer them instead as places from which to begin a personal, school-specific journey.

We want to emphasize that ways of beginning journeys toward learning community schools can be so diverse that the only necessary requirements for those who undertake them are (1) a sense of direction, (2) a willingness to try, and (3) an understanding that the efforts are first steps toward continuous change, not the replacement of what is with an already defined better way—that is, a recognition that the vision on the horizon is not an already built structure. So the journeys can include any efforts by professionals who want to get better at what they do. They do not have to be parts of coordinated endeavors as long as all those pursued in a particular school setting are headed in the same general direction. The individual beginning efforts do, however, have to have recognizable points of intrusion, places of departure, and vehicles for change—that is, means for making them more than single step changes.

Illustrations of Small-Scale Beginning Efforts

We suggest the activities described below as illustrations of small-scale efforts that can be first steps toward creating learning community schools as long as (1) they are developed and pursued continuously over time and (2) they change the thinking of those involved toward that which is appropriate for continuous learning.

• A grade-level group of teachers decides to study collaboratively the learning needs of several of their difficult-to-teach students. (Some would call this collaboration action research.) In weekly needs assessment meetings, they discuss the difficulties of one learner from each teacher's class. They brainstorm about teaching approaches and strategies that might be successful with each student, and they settle on the ones that seem to be most viable for each student. Each teacher tries the recommended strategies with his or her targeted student. At the next week's meeting, each teacher reports on what happened and future plans are set. As the needs assessment meetings continue over time, the teaching of all participants becomes more problem identifying and problem solving in orientation.

• The faculty and administrators decide to pursue the idea of teacher-as-the-first-line-of-service-provider by building all in-service teacher education activities around the expressed instructional needs of teachers. At the start of the school year, each teacher lists up to three things that he or she needs most to improve his or her teaching. The collective needs are identified as the school's highest priority for improvement. All professional development money and time for the year are devoted to meeting these priorities. At the end of the year, the developmental activities are assessed in terms of how they led to improved teaching and better student learning. Teacher journals, test scores, and informal assesments of attitudes could all be examined. Then these results are used to establish the next year's priorities.

- Individual teachers recognize that they are so isolated from one another that they fail to take advantage of each other's expertise and support. They carve out of each school week times when those at each grade level can observe one of their colleagues in a manner similar to the medical rounds of physicians in teaching hospitals. The observed lessons are videotaped for wider viewing, discussion, and critique. Teachers take turns being observed and critiqued. Over time the "teaching rounds" process becomes a common school practice. Teachers learn from each other and increase their respect and understanding of each other.

- An entire school professional community decides to operationalize the belief that every student in the school is the shared, common responsibility of all teachers. They post in the faculty lounge a long blank sheet of paper with the heading, "Students Worthy of Special Attention" and each teacher is asked to record at least one student name and explain why the student needs the extra attention. Each student whose name is listed is then discussed by small groups of teachers and one teacher volunteers to provide the special help agreed on. What happens in each situation is discussed routinely. When a need appears to have been addressed successfully, the student's name is ceremoniously removed from the list and the helping teacher is publicly commended by his or her peer professionals. As a result, sentiments of mutual caring and shared responsibilities for students' needs among teachers creep into the school's professional norms.

- A number of teacher colleagues decide to analyze their classroom practices more closely, develop a plan to experiment with particular teaching strategies, implement the plan, draw conclusions from the results, share their experiment and conclusions with other colleagues, and encourage others to conduct similar experiments. The group repeats this type of experimentation on a regular basis and reports results as a part of its regular teaching activity. Gradually, the teachers integrate this type of classroom experimentation into their norms of practice. They become investigative scholar practitioners.

• An elementary language arts team of teachers decides to focus its professional improvement efforts for the year on a joint plan to teach whole language as best they can. In place of in-service education sessions that would have been arranged for them, teachers organize their own sessions around the project, secure their own outside resource people, plan cooperative lessons, observe and debrief each other, and improve their teaching jointly. As the project develops, teacher learning becomes a regular part of what the teachers do cooperatively and it occurs on school time. Old-style in-service programs gradually disappear.

• About halfway through the school year, the school's teachers and administrators decide to build a stronger sense of community among their teachers and students. They ask all students in the graduating class to write a private and personal thank you note to every teacher they have had during their time at the school. They ask them to include what they are thankful for and why. Then the notes are collected and bound for each teacher. The bound sets are given to the teachers on graduation night, on stage. Every teacher is asked to do the same for every graduating student; those bound notes are given out with diplomas.

A Possible Schoolwide Experiment

For educators who might be interested in a full-school—or a multischool—leap from a traditional school environment to a learning community environment closer to that of our envisioned school on the horizon, we suggest this possibility.

Everyone in a school—or cluster of closely knit schools—agrees formally to work on two mutual goals for an entire school year: (1) continue providing the best possible learning experiences for all students, presumably as has been the case for years, and (2) add to that goal a noticeable movement toward a learning community ideal for every individual school community professional.

Everyone pursues the second goal simultaneously on two levels as follows:

On the individual and small group level:

• Each professional identifies one way he or she will improve during the school year in terms of each of the four dimensions of learning community schools that we have described—morally based learning community, constructivist learning, investigative problem-identifying and problem-solving teaching, and practice-based teacher learning.

- Everyone organizes into mutual support groups of two or more individuals who either have overlapping goals or normally would work closely together anyway.
- Each individual or group identifies four target behaviors or results that will show at the end of the year whether each of the four goals has been met.

For the whole school:

- The full school faculty identifies a way in which the school as a whole will improve during the school year in terms of each of the four dimensions.
- Identifies what will be done to improve in each of the four ways.
- Divides and accepts specific subtasks.
- Identifies target results that will show at the end of the school year if each of the four goals has been reached by the school as a whole.

Both sets of goals—the individual, small group ones and the full-school ones—are written out and posted for all to see all year.

Colleagues monitor progress of each other and the progress of the school as a whole (using devices such as "critical fiends," peer coaching, and mentoring) both continuously and at three or four formally set times during the year.

Everyone helps everyone pursue the goals.

Appropriate adjustments are made along the way.

Everyone keeps personal journals of the getting-better experiences.

At the end of the school year, colleagues evaluate each other and the school effort as a whole by:

- Assessing how well the goals were achieved
- Determining what should be done for the next year

A schoolwide, self-congratulatory celebration occurs during which volunteers might read excerpts from their journals.

Of course, many of the specifics about how such an experiment should be conducted would be decided on locally, but these decisions and how they are made and acted on are central to the getting-better journey. We have described our views of the destination but sketched only a vague picture of the path. There is no road map. The journey is an experiment.

Larger-Scale Reform Efforts That Can Be Vehicles for Change

The activities of many better known and positively evaluated current education reform projects and consortia can serve as examples of points of departure and vehicles for change for schools seeking to become learning communities, and using them as such begins by learning about them and selecting from among them. In our view, those that are most helpful are the ones whose thrust and focus are consistent with (1) the interests and motivation of a particular community's participants at all levels—not just the individuals in positions of authority; (2) the conditions at which that school community finds itself at the start of the getting-better endeavor; and (3) the vision, images, and goals that the community has identified for itself. The way in which a project's activities are used by the school community is critical, however. Using them as models or exemplars—as already defined and constructed structures on the horizon—to be replicated would contradict our ideas of building learning communities and, we believe, not work. Using them as devices to prod thinking, learning, movement toward a particular school community's personally identified images of what it could and should become would be on target. The task is to build a learning community; the project and consortia examples are means for doing so, not models of what a particular school should become.

Below we present information about several projects and consortia whose activities we think can serve as sources of ideas for both points of departure and vehicles for change.

— The *Coalition of Essential Schools* is a national school reform movement begun in the mid-1980s under the leadership of Theodore R. Sizer of Brown University. It focuses on high schools and is based on nine common principles of better schooling:

1. The school should focus on helping adolescents learn to use their minds well.

2. The school's goal should be simple: Each student masters a limited number of essential skills and areas of knowledge.

3. The school's goals should apply to all students; the means to these goals will vary as those students themselves vary.

4. Teaching and learning should be personalized to the maximum feasible extent.

5. The governing practical metaphor of the school should be student-as-worker rather than the more familiar metaphor of teacher-as-deliverer-of-instructional-services.

6. Students entering secondary school studies are those who can show competence in language and elementary mathematics.

7. The tone of the school should explicitly and self-consciously stress values of unanxious expectation of trust and decency. Incentives appropriate to the school's particular students and teachers should be emphasized, and parents should be treated as essential collaborators.

8. The principal and teachers should perceive themselves as generalists first and specialists second.

9. Teacher loads should not exceed 80 students; substantial time should be provided for collective planning by teachers; salaries should be competitive and the ultimate per pupil cost should not exceed that at traditional schools by more than 10%. (Muncey & McQuillan, 1996, pp. 2-3).

> Muncey and McQuillan (1996), Chapter 1, provides a clear and concise description of the coalition; subsequent chapters offer insights on how ideas from the coalition could be used to pursue learning community goals. Additional information can be obtained from Susan Fisher, Publications Department, Coalition of Essential Schools, Box 1969, Brown University, Providence, RI 02912; phone 401-863-3384; Web site: http://www.ces.brown.edu.

— *Accelerated schools* is a national school restructuring movement established formally in 1986 by Henry M. Levin of Stanford University. Its general purpose is to enable schools to replace remediation plans for students at risk of failure with school cultures that accelerate learning for all students. Key project principles are unity of purpose, empowerment coupled with responsibility, and building on strengths (Finnan, St. John, McCarthy, & Slovacek, 1996, p. 15).

> Finnan et al. (1996) provide an overview, background, and explanation of the ideas central to the project. Additional information can be obtained from the National Center for Accelerated Schools Project, Stanford University, CERAS 109, Stanford, CA 94305-3084; Web site: http//www-leland.stanford.edu/group/asp/.

— The *League of Professional Schools* is a network of schools engaged in school-initiated and teacher-driven reform. It is based on reform ideas of Carl Glickman of the University of Georgia, including the principle that problems in public education can be solved best at the school level. Its three guiding premises are shared governance, action research, and instructional focus (Glickman, 1993).

> Two articles that provide information about the ideas and work of the league are Glickman (1992) and Allen and Glickman (1992). Additional information can be obtained from the League of Professional Schools, The University of Georgia, College of Education, Aderhold Hall, Athens, GA 30603.

— *School Power,* also known as the *School Development Project,* began initially as a collaboration among the Yale University Child Study Center; the New Haven, Connecticut, schools; parents; and communities concerned about the need for school success for poor and hard-to-teach students. It is based on the ideas of Yale psychologist James P. Comer, its founder and leader. Over the past two decades, it has been used as a model nationwide. The approach calls for the following:

1. Organizing schools around concepts from child development, particularly social development
2. Building a sense of community among all school stakeholders—teachers, administrators, students, parents, and so forth
3. Drawing all who provide services to students—teachers, administrators, psychologists, social workers—into a team that

addresses student needs and responds systematically, rather than in isolation from each other

4. Close school-parent cooperation

5. An instructional emphasis on student social skills development through a program called "A Social Skills Curriculum for Inner-City Children" (Comer, 1980)

> Comer (1980, 1993) and Comer, Haynes, Joyner, and Ben-Avie (1996) describe the approach and its implementation. Additional information can be obtained from Cynthia Savo, School Development Program, 52 College Street, New Haven, CT 06510; Web site: http://info.med.yale.edu/comer/welcome.html.

— *Professional development school* (PDS) arrangements now number in the hundreds and many of their activities—but by no means all—can be useful as points of departure and vehicles for change. General and specific information about PDSs is plentiful and found in many sources, including the following: most issues of the newspaper *Education Week*; Darling-Hammond (1994); Levine (1992); Petrie, (1995); Levine and Trauchtman (1997); Teitel and Del Prete (1995); various publications of the Clinical Schools Clearinghouse, American Association of Colleges for Teacher Education; and publications of the National Center for Restructuring Education, Schools, and Teaching, Teachers College, Columbia University.

> The three university PDS organizations described briefly below engage in particular efforts that can provide examples of good starting points.

- Ohio State University has multiple PDS arrangements with schools and school districts in the Columbus, Ohio, area; the individual arrangements are rather autonomous and varied. At their core, all intend to link teacher education students and teacher educators at the university with faculty, administrators, and students in schools. Some focus on schools and student learning in general ways, others concentrate on instruction across the curriculum, and still others have more specific subject focuses. A particularly informative document about Ohio State efforts is *Anatomy of a Professional Development School*

Initiative (1993), a profile prepared for the annual meeting of the American Association of Colleges for Teacher Education. Additional information about Ohio State PDS collaborations can be obtained from Office of the Dean, College of Education, Arps Hall, 1945 North High, The Ohio State University, Columbus, OH 43210.

- The University of Cincinnati has two collaborative arrangements with local schools: a Professional Practice Schools partnership with the city of Cincinnati and the Cincinnati Federation of Teachers; and a newer PDS relationship with several suburban Cincinnati school districts. Both efforts are clearly structured and focus on a year-long induction of graduate students as new teachers. Both are good examples of collaborative professional development among a university, school, and teacher leaders. Information can be obtained from The Cincinnati Initiative for Teacher Education, 603 Teachers College, College of Education, University of Cincinnati, Cincinnati, OH 45221; phone: 513-556-3612.

- The Southern Maine Partnership is a consortium of the University of Southern Maine, Maine College of Art, Southern Maine Technological College, 27 local school districts, and 2 independent schools. It focuses its activities on teacher development and student learning needs as identified by Partnership participants. It is affiliated with both the National Education Association (NEA) Professional Development Schools Network and the National Network for Educational Renewal. Information can be obtained from the Southern Maine Partnership, College of Education and Human Development, University of Southern Maine, 117 Bailey Hall, Gorham, ME 04038, phone: 207-780-5498.

— Schools affiliated with the *Center for Educational Renewal* and the *National Network for Educational Renewal,* University of Washington, are partners in a nationwide network of university-school collaboratives that, in effect, make them PDSs. The center and the network have evolved since the 1980s under the leadership of John I. Goodlad and have been influenced significantly by the ideas of the Holmes Group. One particularly viable renewal collaboration is the Brigham Young University Public School Partnership.

Goodlad (1994a), Osguthorpe, Harris, Harris, and Black (1995), Clark (1992), and Goodlad (1994b) provide much general information about Center for Renewal schools and how they work. Additional information can be obtained from the National Network for Educational Renewal, University of Washington, Seattle, WA 98145, and from the Office of the Dean, College of Education, Brigham Young University, Provo, UT 84602.

— Three especially active clearinghouses and networks for securing ideas and information about school reform efforts in schools throughout the United States are the following:

- The Clinical Schools Clearing House, American Association of Colleges for Teacher Education, One Dupont Circle, Suite 610, Washington, DC 20036

- The National Center for Restructuring Education, Schools and Teaching, Box 110, Teachers College, Columbia University, 525 W. 120th St., New York, NY 10027

- The Massachusetts Field Center for Teaching and Learning, Wheatley Hall, University of Massachusetts-Boston, 100 Morrissey Blvd., Boston, MA 02125

The NEA is engaged in a number of school-level endeavors that can provide ideas for developing learning committees. Among them are the following:

— The NEA *Teacher Education Initiative* is a national collaboration, begun in 1994, among the NEA, colleges of education, and pre-K-12 schools. The focus for the Teacher Education Initiative is the improvement of the professional development of teachers. The project settings are pre-K-12 PDSs. The program expands the concept of teacher training and retraining through a unique, equitable partnership among schools, universities, and the NEA. The initiative aims to accelerate the pace of change and renewal in teacher preparation and practice, improve the quality of teacher professional development, and produce better performing students. Specifically, this collaborative functions as a unifying element that guides, supports, and facilitates significant improvement in the preparation and induction of new teachers, the continuous

professional growth of all educators, and the research and development of the teaching profession.

The Teacher Education Initiative is organized around nine principles or criteria for the pursuit of quality and renewal identified by
an advisory committee comprising NEA staff, pre-K-12 teachers,
and teacher education leaders:

1. Partnerships with pre-K-12 schools where all stakeholders are
   involved

2. Expanded roles for university and pre-K-12 educators

3. Ongoing evaluation, dissemination, and contributions to the
   professional knowledge base by all stakeholders

4. Extended clinical experiences, mentoring and support for beginning teachers, and systemic professional development for
   experienced teachers

5. Systemic change at the local, state, and national levels

6. Systemic change internally that rewards simultaneous renewal
   efforts

7. Infusion of technology at all levels

8. Advancement of diversity and equity

9. Teaching and learning linked to student outcomes

— The *NEA Charter School Initiative,* a joint project between the
   NEA's National Center for Innovation and its Center for the Advancement of Public Education that began in 1996 in six schools,
   is both a school development project and a network that encour-
   ages teachers to develop charter schools that meet 10 NEA-formu-
   lated criteria. The NEA is also using the project schools as a way
   to determine the efficacy of the charter model to bring innovation
   to the broader system of public education. Overriding themes
   around which the schools operate are student achievement,
   teacher development, and community involvement. The schools
   use eight questions as guides and indicators of achievement:

1. How are these schools adding to our understandings about
   what students should know and be able to do? Are these students learning what they need to know? What are the implications for practice?

2. How are community stakeholders (e.g. parents, businesses, higher education institutions, the broader local community, professional teachers' associations) engaged in the charter school?

3. How are the issues of accountability and governance of schooling worked out in the charter schools?

4. How are the economic benefits, rights, and professional status of charter employees affected by the creation of charter schools in this district?

5. What support or obstacles do funding mechanisms (including start-up funding) present to charter founders?

6. What can be learned from these individual efforts that would inform district, state, and national efforts to improve schooling?

7. How can a productive partnership be developed among the local, state, and national affiliates of the professional teachers' association to improve public education?

8. What does it take to create a new school (e.g., founder characteristics, motivation, planning processes, resource acquisition, obstacles to overcome, and so forth)?

> More information can be obtained from the Teacher Education Initiative, NEA National Center for Innovation, NEA, 1201 16th St., NW, Washington, DC 20036; phone: 202-822-7906.

Now that we have pointed out examples of ideas and activities that we think can stimulate the kind of thinking that can begin and advance the formulation of learning community schools, we feel obligated to end this chapter with two reminders: (1) although others' ideas and actions can stimulate learning community thinking, using them as models to be imported to a local setting absolutely contradicts learning community thinking; and (2) learning communities are built by the ideas and work of individual school teachers, administrators, students, and parents who work together for common goals—not by outsiders.

CHAPTER FIVE

Monitoring, Assessing, and Celebrating

How can we know that we are succeeding?

It is probably obvious by now that our views of the ideal school run counter to the ways in which schools typically function today; to many of the major trends in school change, reform, restructuring, and improvement; and to the dominant education culture of assessment, evaluation, and accountability. It is probably equally evident that, although all schools need to be assessed, if schools are going to be different in the ways we suggest, they need to be assessed and evaluated differently. This chapter looks at this different way of assessing schools, particularly learning community schools. First, we describe our perspective on assessing the kinds of schools we envision; then, we discuss two types of standards that can be used for such assessing: (1) standards based on the four dimensions of our vision of schools on the horizon, and (2) other parallel standards being used by education reformers that we think fit the purpose of making schools better. We suggest the second type—the parallel standards—not so much as alternatives to those that we tie directly to the four dimensions of the schools we envision but as supplements to them.

 A Different Perspective on Assessment

The assessing that is appropriate for making schools, including learning community schools, better needs to be a continuous process of monitoring and checking on how much and what kind of progress is being made toward a school's identified goals. It is not a public re-porting of a final result—not a declaration that a school, teacher, or student has achieved a level of success higher than others in a com-petition or has reached a finish line first and in record time. It is more like the record keeping about athletes in practice than the final score at the end of a championship game.

Monitoring Progress

The kind of assessing that is needed stresses

- Progress more than final results
- Improvement more than measurement
- Responsibility more than competition
- Shared effort more than individual success
- Self-satisfaction more than public acclaim
- Accomplishment more than accountability

For the most part, it compares where an individual school community stands on a particular measure against where it should be and wants to be, rather than against the comparative positions of another school or schools. It is an activity that is part and parcel of a continuous, broad, and developing getting-better effort, not an accounting-type tabulation or a popularity contest. It does not designate winners over losers. The competition that exists is mostly internal and matched against individ-ual goals. There is no victory, no declared finish line—just learners, teachers, and those who support their making progress in comparison to the relative positions of their own work, status, and accomplish-ments of earlier times. Although there may be many successes along the way, these successes are intermediate marks of progress, not evi-dence that tasks are completed or goals are reached—the tasks keep expanding and the goals keep rising.

Comparison With the Ideal

Of course, assessing means comparing and comparing re-quires standards against which the comparison can be made; all com-parison, if it is to have meaning, cannot be internal. Also, the standards against which a school or the components of a school are matched must be seen as valid, worthy of accomplishment, and appropriate. They must represent a hoped-for ideal that school stakeholders want for their school. They must show what has been accomplished and how much more of a need for accomplishment lies ahead.

Student academic achievement and the quality of teaching can illustrate this point. It is probably safe to say that all school community stakeholders believe that schools exist to create learning and that they want the students in their schools to learn as much as they can and the teachers to teach as well as can be expected. So they constantly want to know, How are our students and teachers doing? They want to know if the planned-for and expected learning and teaching are taking place.

This is as it should be. Those who care about a school should want to know if it is accomplishing its purposes satisfactorily. But there is also a danger in this need to know—a danger that overemphasizes accountability, tabulation-type measurement, and test results. This danger sees assessment data as proof that something good or bad has already occurred instead of as indications of how much progress has been made so far and how much still needs to be made. It equates assessment with achievement and achievement with success; then it considers having success as something akin to having completed the task. A more accurate and more useful idea of assessment sees it as the monitoring and reporting of progress—and progress is not quite the same thing as either achievement or success.

When assessing is thought of as a continuous monitoring of progress and it is applied in that light to learning community schools, it can be guided primarily by at least two levels of questions. On the first, and lower, level are questions such as,

- What are our students' achievement test scores?
- How well educated are our teachers?
- How many continuing education workshops have our teachers attended?
- What new, cutting-edge programs have we adopted?
- How does all this compare to neighbor schools and national norms?

But these lower-level questions do not provide final answers to how well a school is doing. They only supply data that have to be interpreted so that higher-level questions can be engaged, questions that call for judgments that compare what is happening with the community's mission, goals, and expectations. Questions such as,

- Are our students learning what and as much as we want them to learn?
- Are they getting better at learning?
- Are we teaching what we want to teach, in the ways we want, and at the level of quality that we want?
- Are we getting better as teachers?
- Are we functioning as a moral, interdependent community?
- Is our mission a good one?
- Does it guide and direct all our activities as well and as consistently as it should?
- Are we becoming better as a community?
- Is our learning as teachers and school professionals developing as it should?

Doing the Assessing

What does all this mean as we attempt to assess our learning community schools? What guidance does it provide as we monitor their progress? What might the assessing task look like? Where should we start and how should we proceed? We suggest the following steps:

1. Start with the four dimensions of our vision and set goals to be sought that apply to each.
2. Design means or paths of action that will move us toward these goals.
3. Identify mileposts along each of the paths that will reflect our progress.
4. Decide what the data from the milepost monitoring mean in terms of our vision and goals.
5. Adjust appropriate facets of our community getting-better endeavor that we believe will enhance our progress in the future.

It is probably apparent that these steps are similar to the steps outlined when we suggested how learning communities can be developed and continuously evolved toward more perfect representations of our vision on the horizon. This is understandable. If developing community, learning, and teaching are all evolutionary processes and if we follow the ideals we are seeking, assessment is simply a matter of determining where we are at a particular time and how well we are progressing. In general terms, the day-to-day assessing of learning communities can be based on two communitywide activities:

1. Setting and adjusting goals consistent with the four dimensions of the community's vision on the horizon
2. Continuously determining where the community and all its components are in pursuit of these goals

The assessing needs to be thorough, honest, and understood by all community stakeholders, including citizens and political leaders who seem to be on the outside looking in. And it must be consistent with, supportive of, and tied to the kinds of things important to those who make up the learning community. If it is not, the priorities internal to the learning community will succumb to external pressures to perform to others' standards in a climate of traditional assessment by comparison and a bean-counting accountability.

Addressing Others' Expectations

We must recognize that all schools, including the learning community schools that we envision, cannot focus so exclusively on their own visions, goals, and internal priorities—students, teachers, administrators, and parents who make up the learning community—that they fail to pay attention to some of the interests of those external to the school. Although these external interests—those of school boards, central office administrators, state agencies, politicians, media, and so forth—may sometimes be constricting and even inhibiting in what they expect of schools, those who hold these interests are stakeholders, their concerns may be legitimate, and their voices need to be heard. If they overvalue narrow approaches to assessments, such as by relying only on achievement test scores or scores on local exit examinations, they need to be educated and persuaded to accept the learning community ideal, at least to the point that they allow learning community participants the freedom to pursue their expertise, goals, priorities, and visions.

If we want to create and nurture school communities characterized by the qualities discussed throughout this book, we need to be clear about our own ideas and means of assessment and then take advantage of the latitude available to us. When all learning community participants accept responsibility for their community and all its work and we all have an honest confidence in our own measures of performance, we can convey that sense of responsibility and confidence to others and even stimulate an acceptance by outsiders of the professional competence and authority that all community members possess. When this happens, questions such as, How did the students do on the examination? can be superseded by questions more pertinent to the ideals and interests we have described thus far—questions such as,

- How do we know that we have a good school, community ethos, instructional programs, and teachers?
- How do we maintain our confidence?
- How do we show this to others convincingly?
- How do we gain and keep their trust?
- How do we know and show others that we are getting better in terms of each of our four dimensions?

In essence,

- How do we know and prove to others that we are doing school right and accomplishing the things that we, and they, think are important?
- How do we know and prove to others that we are a learning community?
- How do we know and prove to others that our students—as well as all of us—are learning as best as they and we can?

Behind all these questions are others more focused and more specific to the assessing process: What do we educators need and wish to know to determine if we are doing school right? What kinds of information should we seek? What kinds of questions will help us find out more about ourselves as educators and ourselves and our students as learners? What do we want to learn regarding parents that will allow our community to develop in more educative ways? What kinds of questionnaires, forms, interviews, and observations do we need to help us gather the information we want? Who can help us obtain, analyze, interpret, synthesize, and disseminate these kinds of information?

Departing from the currently dominant accountability culture in the ways we have just implied can be risky and it might be impossible in some schools, in certain school districts, and under particular conditions. Even the so-called impossible can occur, however, when community professional educators collaborate with parents, central office personnel, school boards, and all community partners to change the perceptions of what school can be and, in turn, what needs to be assessed and evaluated.

Alliances With Parents

Perhaps the key initial alliance in this regard—after formulating a consensus among all onsite learning community professionals and support staff—is assuring parents that what community professional educators want is in the best interests of their children and we are open to their ideas, suggestions, guidance, and participation (Goodlad, 1994b; Sergiovanni, 1996). This process of assuring parents is easier if parents or their representatives are welcomed community participants in a true sense—involved in discussions and decision making with teachers and administrators on school matters of all kinds and personally bonded with other members of the community—if they are cognitively and emotionally involved stakeholders. With an honest teacher-parent alliance in place, the nucleus of a community is formed. Parents, teachers, students, and school administrators and staff members develop commonalties, understanding about each other, and caring for one another. Community bonds grow. Individuals accept membership, develop loyalty, and feel wanted. The school becomes our school. More and more people accept increasing responsibility and more visible stakeholding. Visions considered impossible in factory-model schools become possibilities. All those involved do not just go to school; they belong to it.

The Transition Is Not Easy

This scenario implies an ease of transition from traditional school settings to learning communities that is not realistic. The change in mission, ethos, sentiment, mutual associations, and all that relates to these multiple elements of a community is difficult, uneven, and demanding of energy and time. It involves building community, not adding surface appearances or false facades. Undoubtedly, the most challenging situations will need to be attended to longer and worked at harder than those that already have key supporters and policies in place. But with appropriate democratic procedures, discussion, information, data, workshops, planning, and perseverance, we can be realistically optimistic that major changes are possible if the seeds of a learning community have been sown and all appropriate subgroups are dedicated to making significant changes. We make these remarks being fully cognizant of the stifling bureaucratic mazes, the dictatorial personality types, and the self-defeating behavior that works against us on occasion. We remain optimistic because we think the overwhelming majority of people want children to grow, mature, and learn and want professional educators to be successful and satisfied in their professional roles.

In keeping with our prior thoughts that there are no exemplars of perfectly compatible models that fit all communities, schools, or situations, we acknowledge that there is no single way to find out how students, teachers, and parents can best grow and learn. We also freely admit that our four-dimensional vision of what school communities should be like should not be seen as an exclusive standard for assessing progress even for the kinds of schools we advocate. On the contrary, we can learn from others' ways of determining quality in schools, and knowing about these other ideas and putting them into use alongside those that we have developed from our particular perspective can enhance our efforts to improve schools and save valuable time and energy. We ought to know what other leaders of school reform and improvement already know as well as what they already have done, and have done well.

Therefore, we describe below five images that others have used in recent years as standards against which to measure how good schools are—both the schools that they work with directly and schools in general. We think all five provide useful parallel standards for assessing learning communities. They complement our beacons on the horizon in the distance.

Assessment Using Other Parallel Standards

In this time when nearly everyone who cares about schools wants to know how well schools are doing in educating their students, it is important that schools be judged by more than one set of criteria.

Therefore, the learning community schools that we envision should be assessed by more criteria and standards than those embodied in our own vision of schools on the horizon. Parallel standards should be used to answer the questions, How good are our schools? How can we be sure of this? By what standards are they being judged? We suggest five alternative images of schools that include criteria and standards that can be used to address these questions in addition to the standards incorporated into our four-dimensional vision of learning communities.

- The satisfied school
- The growing school
- The virtuous, convenantal school
- The good school
- The achieving school

Before we turn to these descriptions and explanations, however, we need to warn that we are about to intermix *ideas, guides,* and *standards* and to use the same labels for all three. For example *satisfied school* is a label for (1) an idea and ideal we may want to pursue, (2) a guide that directs our pursuing of the ideal, and (3) a standard for determining whether our school communities are as close to the ideal as we would like. Three reminders are also in order: First, these five images of quality schools and school communities are not mutually exclusive; second, what is meant by each label needs to be made as clear as possible if it is to be useful as a standard of quality—ambiguous visions and ideals can guide us to some extent but ambiguous standards are significantly less useful; and third, each standard has to be adjusted to fit local circumstances and conditions before it can serve as an evaluative standard for judging any specific school. So, what do we mean by these labels and how can the images portrayed by them be described clearly enough to make them useful as standards?

The Satisfied School

For an idea about a satisfied school, we turn to John Goodlad (1994a), who observes that in nearly every area of life except schooling, people's satisfaction with an experience or product is deemed important. For example, products and services are almost uniformly viewed as good if customers like what they get and salespeople like what they sell. In contrast, little or no evaluative credibility is given to the views of parents, students, and teachers on satisfaction surveys. In fact, reports that schools are satisfying to parents, students, and educators are often questioned skeptically and even viewed with suspicion.

Goodlad (1994a) argues, and we agree, that the question of how we determine whether a school is good or not—he uses *good* to mean as good as it can be—needs to be examined closely and he uses the idea of satisfaction as a key determinate of goodness. He concludes from his research that there is a high correlation between the degree of satisfaction of three groups—students, teachers, and parents—and external indicators of quality, such as independent observations by observers and achievement test scores. He also says there is a similar correlation when students, teachers, and parents are dissatisfied with their schools (pp. 207-211). This seems only logical. Students, teachers, and parents are unlikely to be satisfied with dull, out-of-control, and unproductive schools; and it is not likely that these three groups would independently concur that schooling is being done well if planning of, engaging in, and learning from educative experiences is not occurring.

Based on his findings, Goodlad (1994a) suggests seven general characteristics of good schools:

1. Good schools are good in nearly all realms—they function well from beginning to end—and poor schools are genuinely poor throughout.

2. The goodness of schools is partially influenced by the conditions of the broader school district. Good schools both help form and are formed by good districts.

3. Good schools are characterized by time for reflection and self-consciousness. (We would add an understanding of and a commitment to vision.) The school understands itself and directs its time and energies to acting on principle and policy rather than reacting to problems and coping with crises.

4. Good schools understand their business and take care of it in orderly and predictable ways, whereas poor schools are run in ad hoc fashion with a great deal of ambiguity about responsibilities.

5. Good schools are characterized by understanding and valuing the importance of educative and academic experiences. Poor schools seem to have lost sight of academic goals.

6. Good schools are generally positive in their interpersonal relationships among professionals and between professionals and students—principals, teachers, and students usually enjoy one another and their interactions.

7. Good schools have positive linkages with parents—school professionals know parents and parents know the staff, they have mutual interests and are involved with and respect each other (pp. 212-214).

In light of this research by Goodlad (1994a), satisfied schools can be described as schools that concentrate on things within the power of teachers, principals, students, and parents. They focus on the conditions that they can influence by ensuring that

1. The whole and not just the parts of the school are cared for
2. The district is influenced by the school in a positive direction
3. A reflective and self-conscious culture is nurtured
4. The orderly care of school business is attended to
5. The importance of academic matters is sustained
6. The cultivation of positive interpersonal relationships is pursued
7. The development of school-home interactions is prized

It is important to point out that, although Goodlad (1994a) equates satisfied and good, his use of the term *satisfied* should not be interpreted to mean that students, professional educators, and parents of satisfied schools do not want their schools to get better and expect them to do so. He speaks directly and forcefully about school improvement and the need of school community participants to cultivate the conditions that lead to greater satisfaction. It would be more appropriate to say that Goodlad envisions a satisfied school as one in which satisfaction includes the fact that the school and all involved in it are continuing to grow and develop—an idea explored in the next section of this chapter.

This getting-better aspect of a satisfied school is reinforced by Goodlad's (1994a) observation that in good (satisfied) schools, teachers make professional decisions and experiment or, as Goodlad describes it, their principals allow them the freedom to teach in keeping with their professional judgments. The principals respect their professional staffs and permit them to practice what they believe is merited (pp. 211-217).

The Growing School

When we look beyond the satisfied school, as Goodlad (1994a) describes it, for a standard to help us assess our educational endeavors, we can move in a variety of directions but perhaps none is more important than that suggested by John Dewey (1916/1944, 1938/1963). Although Dewey probably would have supported much of Goodlad's notion of a satisfied school, he stresses more than Goodlad the need for school communities to grow, and his ideas of growth are integrally related to his view of *educative experiences.* For Dewey, there are three kinds of experiences: educative, noneducative, and miseducative. Educative experiences are those that involve growth in themselves and lead to further growth. Noneducative and miseducative experiences do not involve growth and do not lead to further opportunities for growth. In fact, miseducative experiences actually inhibit or limit additional growth.

But what does *growth* mean as Dewey (1916/1944, 1938/1963) uses the term, and how do we know when it is occurring in a school? First, we should mention that Dewey's concept of the person as a social being, as well as paralleling ideas expressed by Jean Piaget, Lawrence Kohlberg, Lev Vygotsky, and others, means that a person grows socially and cognitively by interacting with others—a phenomenon that is particularly significant in and for a learning community. This means that the growth of one person or subgroup in a school affects the learning and growth of others. This in turn means that the goal of growth—and thus the assessing of growth—is both individual and communitywide.

Second, Dewey's concept of growth includes a cognitive focus— learning how to learn and how to think reflectively. He speaks often (1933/1960) of the ability to think reflectively or scientifically—being able and inclined to give careful consideration to evidence and argument—when addressing personal, social, and intellectual problems. Here he is distinguishing the educated person by his or her disposition to think reflectively about life, rather than responding from a blind adherence to tradition, ideology, or opinion.

Dewey envisions a society or community in which alternatives are decided on the basis of the best available evidence and strongest reasoned arguments, giving due consideration to the strengths and weaknesses of various positions. He advocates that educators, students, and citizens analyze their beliefs to determine if they are warranted and if they should be acted on. He particularly wants people to recognize that beliefs and behaviors supported only by unexamined customs, feelings, and assumptions and not open to criticism are detrimental to educative discussions and experiences in schools and the broader community. Thus, he argues (1938/1963) that we can avoid being dogmatic only by being willing and disposed to evaluate every point of view on the basis of relevant evidence and argument.

Dewey (1956/1990) also thinks growing involves using our capacities to communicate, construct, inquire, and create in the daily affairs of living and learning, a living that will move beyond immediate enjoyment to include activities in service of the community. He speaks (1909/1975) of the desirable features of life and learning as including (1) developing an appreciation for what one is doing because it is intrinsically related to life, (2) learning to appreciate one's strengths without being pleased that others are weaker in comparison, (3) learning that some things are valuable within themselves and do not always have to prepare someone to do something else, (4) developing the capacity to carry forward from the past those values that made both prior and present experiences worth having, and (5) developing the capacity for cooperative and personal achievement. This service-to-others aspect of Dewey's idea of growth may be an eye-catching one, but, if we think for a moment, we can recognize that our emphases on civic education, character education, or moral education involve the idea that everyone has a responsibility to serve others in ways that make the world a better place to live. For Dewey (1909/1975), all education is moral education, and good education includes growth; consequently, education includes growing in our service to others.

If we use these ideas of Dewey's, growing schools can be described as schools in which everyone—teachers, students, staff, and possibly parents—as individuals and as a community

1. Grow socially and cognitively by interacting with each other

2. Learn how to learn and how to think reflectively

3. Develop an increasing interest in and capacity to be of service to each other and to the community as a whole

It is not sufficient for each of these characteristics to be present in static form. They must be growing and developing.

The Virtuous, Covenantal School

In describing his perspectives of what characterizes quality schools, Thomas Sergiovanni (1992, 1994, 1996) emphasizes the importance of developing what he calls a *virtuous* or *covenantal community*—a community organized around an agreed-on statement of mission, goals, and values that provide its moral authority for schooling. This covenant between educators, students, and parents, Sergiovanni argues, changes the school from a mere organization into a community and shifts its emphasis from external and psychological authority to moral authority. Much like Goodlad and Dewey, Sergiovanni believes that schooling has a moral obligation to design, act on, and measure itself by criteria such as justice, equal respect of persons, concern for the welfare of others, open communication, fairness, empathy, tolerance, impartiality, and compassion.

Much like Goodlad, Sergiovanni (1992, 1994, 1996) summarizes his main points under five generalizations and argues that the schools that have these virtuous features also contribute to the making of an effective school—a school that achieves in the areas of academic learning. His five features of virtue, which can also serve as criteria for assessing the virtuousness of schools, are as follows:

1. The school is an inquiring, curious, and reflective community that nourishes the development of self-learning and management.

2. Everyone in the school believes that every student—and we would add every educator and parent—is a capable learner who needs to have obstacles to his or her learning removed.

3. The school is motivated to meet the needs of every student as a whole person, including their social, emotional, physical, and intellectual development.

4. The school is built on the principle of equal respect of persons, resulting in genuine respect among parents, teachers, students, and administrators.

5. The school community recognizes that in an interdependent community each person has rights and responsibilities, benefits, and obligations.

The Good School

Because *good* is intrinsically a comparative term and an idea used in innumerable different contexts rather than one tied to particular descriptive characteristics, using it to assess schools requires even more clarification than that which is necessary for the labels *satisfied school, growing school,* and *virtuous school.* For example, the Goodlad idea of good school that we discussed takes on a particular meaning as a standard only when it is explained in the context of satisfaction. That is why we use his term *satisfied* rather than *good.* Now we turn to good as a standard of quality for learning community schools. So our initial question has to be, What do we mean by good? In much of the assessing of schools of today, good is equated with academic achievement in certain content areas—usually reading and mathematics—as measured on standardized tests whose scores are compared with the scores of students in other schools. A school is thought to be good when its students' test scores are higher than those of students in most other schools. This point is illustrated, for example, by a series of policy papers produced by the Brookings Institution (*Brookings Papers on Education Policy,* 1997) that address in almost exclusively academic achievement terms the question, What is the real state of education in America today? In similar fashion, a book also by Brookings (Ladd, 1996), *Holding Schools Accountable,* is advertised by a flier that begins,

> How can schools do a better job of educating our children? Despite hundreds of reforms over the past decade, test scores have remained stagnant while per pupil spending has rapidly increased. Many experts believe that any future reforms should focus on the primary mission of elementary and secondary schools.

The primary mission referred to here is, of course, student academic achievement, which is described as "educational outcome." This equating of good with academic achievement and test scores is, in fact, one dimension of a good school, and we discuss achievement as a measure of school quality next.

First, however, we suggest that a good school be thought of more broadly. For us, goodness, in addition to academic learning, has ethical and social dimensions similar to those identified by Goodlad, Dewey, and Sergiovanni and broad pedagogical dimensions that include more than teacher technical proficiency and the characteristics of schools that have come to be known as characteristics of school effectiveness.

In this vein, useful ways of defining and assessing school goodness need to look at how well the school environment—the entire cultural community with all its parts—contributes to the learning and growth of students, educators, support staff, and parents. Criteria can be found to assess good schools in this way by turning to ideas described by two contemporary education writers—to what Max Van Manen (1991) calls "a complex of pedagogical qualities" and what William Hare (1993a, 1993b) suggests as the set of qualities, attitudes, and dispositions that make up "educators' virtues." Although both writers focus primarily on teachers, we think their ideas apply to the entire learning community.

Van Manen (1991) describes his complex of pedagogical qualities as more than the technical abilities of teachers to teach well. They include

- A sense of vocation
- Love and caring for children
- A deep sense of responsibility, moral intuitiveness, self-critical openness, thoughtful maturity, tactful sensitivity toward the child's subjectivity
- An interpretive intelligence
- A pedagogical understanding of the child's needs
- Improvisational resoluteness in dealing with young people
- A passion for knowing and learning the mysteries of the world
- The moral fiber to stand up for something
- A certain understanding of the world
- Active hope in the face of prevailing crises
- Humor and vitality (p. 8)

Hare (1993a, 1993b) identifies eight complementary qualities that he thinks make educators and the communities in which they participate good. When we apply his ideas to learning community schools, we conclude that good school communities should

- Nurture humility on the part of professional educators, students, and parents
- Cultivate moral courage for community members to address sensitive concerns openly

- Encourage impartiality in evaluating different ideas, proposals, events, practices, research, and policies
- Nourish the development of open-mindedness by educators, students, and parents as they examine different perspectives and new evidence
- Advance the growth of empathy by members of the learning community so they become more genuinely concerned with the problems, dilemmas, and difficulties of others
- Nurse a progressive enthusiasm by the entire community of inquirers for knowledge, learning, and teaching
- Promote professional judgment and decision making by educators and evaluative thinking by students and parents
- Support teachers, students, and parents as they use their imagination to renew schools, improve learning, and develop educative experiences (1993b, p. 11)

Hare (1993a) believes, and we concur, that we are all capable of manifesting these virtues to various degrees and we are equally capable of developing vices that strike at the heart of a good learning community. Those who exhibit these vices are arrogant and dismissive rather than humble and eager to learn, particularly in response to students. They fall in with popular trends in their professional work rather than use personal good judgment to direct their practice. They fail to challenge the status quo or to act with courage and imagination. They are often biased and prejudiced rather than impartial and open minded. They are dogmatic and indifferent rather than empathic toward the concerns of others. They treat rules as if they are absolute rather than norms to be applied to specific situations with personal, professional decision making and insight. They are uninspired and uninspiring instead of dreamers and motivators. They lack enthusiasm for what they are doing—their teaching and learning.

Hare (1993a, 1993b) contends that in schools of quality the ideals of good teachers—and we would add other participants as well—are passed on and developed throughout the school community. He implies, therefore, that good schools have good teachers who act on and nurture their identified qualities of goodness and display these virtues when they interact with one another, with students, and with parents. If he is correct and our interpretation is sound, learning communities consist of members who are humble, courageous, impartial, open-minded, empathic, enthusiastic, reflective, and imaginative and who, as a whole unit, design educational experiences that enhance these virtues.

Characteristics such as these suggested by both Van Manen and Hare can be placed alongside academic learning as standards for assessing the goodness of schools. They are qualities, attitudes, and dispositions that need to live and flourish if learning is to occur. They are necessary elements of good schools.

The Achieving School

Although we have touched on achievement several times in this book, including as a standard by which to assess the quality of schools and school communities, we need to mention several points more explicitly.

1. Schools need to be assessed against what they are intending to accomplish—against their mission, their vision, their purposes and goals—and this is, in fact, a measure of achievement. It addresses the question, Is a school achieving what it expects and is expected to achieve? Student learning, including that reflected in measures of academic achievement, is at the core of a learning community's mission, vision, purposes, and goals.

2. The difficulty with the way in which achievement is often assessed today has to do with the narrowness of what is assessed and the narrowness of the data used—comparative scores on single subject tests, for example. We do not question the assessing of achievement broadly defined. Having an achieving school community is a supremely worthy goal as long as it applies to the full mission of the school and its broad range of purposes and goals.

3. In this latter context, an assessment of how well a learning community school is achieving in an academic dimension is a legitimate and appropriate standard—it reports how much learning is taking place. It is not, however, a legitimate, or particularly useful, final result in a supposed competition with other schools.

How Can We Know?

The answer to the question, How can we know we are succeeding? has three parts—parts that focus on direction, progress, and assessment. Before we elaborate, we want to stress several basic assumptions and principles that undergird the question, all parts of our answer to it, and all that we have been saying throughout this book about learning community schools:

- All learning communities are ideas and entities in the process of becoming something better, or more perfect, than they currently are.
- Where any school starts in that process is not a static point—at any time a school is moving, developing, changing.
- It is not useful in that process to declare a school *bad.*
- There is no permanent fixed point in the distance that is labeled *good.*

Because of these principles, our how-can-we-know question can be answered by monitoring and assessing

1. The *direction* in which our learning community is moving
2. The amount and pace of our *progress* in that direction as marked
3. How the point at which our community rests on the path toward getting better at any particular time compares with what we expect and what we should expect

The more specific subquestions that have to be asked to provide the information needed to assess a school community are

- Is our vision of the way learning community schools should be and are our images of all dimensions of that vision correct and appropriate?
- Are we moving toward the images?
- Is our progress adequate?

To secure realistic and useful answers to these three questions, we can turn to four sets of other types of questions—questions that are more focused and have standards embedded in them. Some of the questions are rather general and intended to promote serious reflection and honest discussion among community participants. Others are more specific, particularly those listed under item 2, and intended as guides for the seeking of precise evidence. Taken together, they can be used to determine whether a learning community is succeeding. The four sets of questions are the following:

1. To what extent are we as learning community members
   - Looking toward images or beacons on the horizon, rather than over our shoulders?
   - Building paths toward these beacons?
   - Progressing up these paths at a satisfying rate?
2. To what extent is
   - Our learning community a morally based community of learners with an agreed on mission and an authentic atmosphere for learning?
   - Its learning a pervasive process of intellectual construction?
   - Its teaching investigative problem identification and problem solving?
   - The knowledge, competence, and value perspectives of all its participants the knowledge, competence, and value perspectives of professional practice? (Specific subquestions on each of these four questions appear in Chapter 4.)
3. To what extent is our learning community school
   - Satisfying to all stakeholders?
   - Growing in all dimensions?
   - Virtuous and covenantal?
   - Good in the broad sense that we have been using the term?
   - Achieving what we want it to achieve?
4. To what extent can all who identify with our learning community school feel good about
   - Our mission?
   - Our work?
   - Our colleagues?
   - Our community?
   - Ourselves?

Learning community school participants know they are succeeding when three things are happening: (1) when the community as a whole is continuously getting better at satisfying its mission, (2) when all participants are learning from the process, and (3) when everyone feels good about what they are accomplishing. When all three occur, it is time to celebrate.

 ## Conclusion

The main point we have been advocating in this book is that schools can be made better than they now are by professional-teacher-led, communitywide journeys toward visions of what schools should be, and we have described our own vision of these schools as morally based, mission-driven communities of learners. We have been suggesting that the getting-better journeys can and should be led by informed, ever-investigating community participants of all types dedicated to helping students learn. We see the journeys as evolutionary approaches to revolutionary change—change that results in the creation of inclusive learning environments in which everyone belongs, everyone is responsible, and everyone learns—all the time. We argue that these journeys toward visions on the horizon are more appropriate than the many school improvement, reform, and restructuring efforts that focus on present weaknesses, cast blame, and concentrate on item-by-item remediation.

We do not assume that schools are all bad or that any school is prefect, nor do we assume that any school community will actually reach—or become—the idealized vision that its participants set for themselves; but we do believe that the individual community participants of any school make it what it is at any particular time and can make it better over time—make it what they want it to be. And we believe the making-it-better journeys accomplish at least two things: (1) they move school communities and the learning experiences around which they are organized closer to the ideal, and (2) they establish the community tasks of improving learning and teaching as both dominant school goals and norms.

Our own personal vision of what schools should be—our communities of learners—are cultures in which everyone experiences learning, pursues learning, and achieves learning; everyone belongs and knows it; everyone shares and is committed to a common mission; and everyone strives for the common good. In our vision, everyone learns and likes it. Throughout this book, we have described our vision in terms of four dimensions: (1) school environments recognized as morally based communities of learners; (2) learning that is understood as experience-based intellectual construction; (3) teaching that is approached as investigative problem identification and problem solving; and (4) professional knowledge, competence, and value perspectives developed in practice. We have also explained some of the philosophical principles that undergird our vision, offered suggestions for moving toward it, and described means we think can be used to assess how well each getting-better journey is progressing. We hope the four dimensions of the proposed vision serve as ideas on which education professionals can reflect, ponder, and build their own visions and pursue their own journeys.

At the same time, however, we have tried to be clear in saying that we do not believe that schools can be made as good as they should be by imposing on them or importing for them unmodified models of practice developed by others for other situations. And we caution that that same belief applies for the ideas outlined here. We have been sharing ideas and offering examples, not recommending any preset plans for adoption.

Frankly, we do not think the elements of our image of learning community schools are far removed from scenes, situations, and circumstances that occur in classrooms and schools everyday. In fact, they occur outside as well as inside schools—everywhere learners gather. For example, we see aspects of our learning community ideas when we visit a bookstore where learners of all ages—from 3 years old to those well into their 90s—hang out. They sit for hours from early in the day to well into the night, 7 days a week—on benches, on the stairs, in the aisles—reading, learning. We saw it in a news story several years ago about a nighttime break-in at a Baltimore middle school by students who wanted more time at the computers. We remember it from our own teaching in public schools and at the college level when students voluntarily stay after school or come by the office to talk, question (argue), and think; and when former students write or come back to say they have learned from their experiences with us and our colleagues. We visualize it in our realization that students and teachers depicted in popular films such as *Stand and Deliver, Dead Poets' Society, Conrack,* and *Mr. Holland's Opus* exist in real life and in real learning community schools. We are suggesting only that these scenes, situations, and circumstances become more common and more prevalent—that they become the norms, the expected.

Finally, we think this book is about dreams—visions—and about making those dreams come true for more learners more often. The dreams are happy ones. As teachers, learners, parents, and all others associated with schools, we can make them come true. If we succeed, stories like those about Jaime Escalante, John Keating, Pat Conroy, and Glenn Holland will not be about unusual teachers who fight their colleagues and challenge the system to help students learn. These types of stories will be so common that everyone will have his or her own personal happy learning experience to talk about—personal happy experiences in school. Schools will be communities of learners who want to be where they are—in school—and want to do what they are doing—learning.

Bibliography

Allen, L., & Glickman, C. D. (1992). School improvement: The elusive face of shared governance. *NASSP Bulletin, 76*(542), 80-87.

Anatomy of a professional development school initiative. (1993). Columbus: Ohio State University, Office of the Dean.

Apple, M., & Beane, J. (Eds.). (1995). *Democratic schools.* Alexandria, VA: Association for Supervision and Curriculum Development.

Ball, D. L., & Wilson, S. M. (1996). Integrity in teaching: Recognizing the fusion of the moral and intellectual. *American Educational Research Journal, 33*(1), 155-192.

Barth, R. S. (1988). School: A community of leaders. In A. Lieberman (Ed.), *Building successful cultures in schools* (pp. 129-147). New York: Teachers College Press.

Barth, R. S. (1990). *Improving schools from within: Teachers, parents, and principals can make the difference.* San Francisco: Jossey-Bass.

Bateson, G. (1972). *Steps to an ecology of mind.* San Francisco: Ballantine.

Bateson, M. C. (1994). *Peripheral visions.* New York: HarperCollins.

Beck, L. G., & Murphy, J. (1994). *Ethics in educational leadership programs.* Thousand Oaks, CA: Corwin.

Beck, L. G., & Murphy, J. (1996). *The four imperatives of a successful school.* Thousand Oaks, CA: Corwin.

Bellah, R. N., Madsen, R., Sullivan, W. M., Swindler, A., & Tipton, S. (1985). *Habits of the heart: Individualism and commitment in American life.* New York: HarperCollins.

Berliner, D. C. (1990). If the metaphor fits, why not wear it? The teacher as executive. *Theory into Practice, 29*(2), 85-93.

Binney, G., & Williams, C. (1995). *Leaning into the future: Changing the way people change organizations.* London: Nicholas Brealey.

Blackford, S. (1995). *School improvement and a community of leaders.* Hayward: California State University, Center for Educational Leadership.

Block, P. (1993). *Stewardship: Choosing service over self-interest.* San Francisco: Berrett Koehler.

Bolman, L. G., & Deal, T. E. (1991). *Reframing organizations: Artistry, choice and leadership.* San Francisco: Jossey-Bass.

Bonstingl, J. J. (1992). *Schools of quality: An introduction to total quality management in education.* Alexandria, VA: Association for Supervision and Curriculum Development.

Boyer, E. (1994). The basic school: Focusing on the child. *Principal, 73*(3), 19-32.

Boyer, E. (1995). *The basic school: A community for learning.* Princeton, NJ: The Carnegie Foundation for the Advancement of Teaching.

Bradley, A. (1993). By asking teachers about context of work, center moves to the cutting edge of research. *Education Week, 12*(27), 6-7.

Brandt, R. (1994). On making sense: A conversation with Magdalene Lampert. *Educational Leadership, 51*(5), 26-30.

Bretall, R. (Ed.). (1946). *Kierkegaard anthology.* Princeton, NJ: Princeton University Press.

Britzman, D. P. (1991). *Practice makes practice: A critical study of learning to teach.* Albany: SUNY Press.

Brookings papers on educational policy. (1997). Washington, DC: Brookings Institution.

Brooks, M., & Gernnon-Brooks, J. (1993). *In search of understanding: The case for constructivist classrooms.* Alexandria, VA: Association for Supervision and Curriculum Development.

Brown, A. (1994). The advancement of learning. *Educational Researcher, 23*(8), 4-12.

Bruner, J. S. (1966). *Toward a theory of instruction.* New York: Norton.

Bryk, A. S., & Driscoll, M. E. (1988). *The high school as community: Contextual influences and consequences for students and teachers.* Madison: Wisconsin Center for Education Research.

Canfield, J., & Hansen, M. V. (1993). *Chicken soup for the soul: 101 stories to open the heart and rekindle the spirit.* Deerfield Beach, FL: Health Communications.

Canfield, J., & Hansen, M. V. (1995). *A Second helping of chicken soup for the soul: 101 more stories to open the heart and rekindle the spirit.*Deerfield Beach, FL: Health Communications.

Castle, D. K., & Estes, N. (1994). *High-performance learning communities.*Thousand Oaks, CA: Corwin.

Cawelti, G. (1994). *High school restructuring: A national study.* Arlington, VA: Educational Research Services.

Chase, B. (1997, February). *Speech before the National Press Club.* Washington, DC.

Clandinin, D. J., & Connelly, F. M. (1987). Teachers' personal knowledge: What counts as "personal" in studies of the personal. *Journal of Curriculum Studies, 19*(6), 487-500.

Clandinin, D. J. & Connelly, F. M. (1995). *Teachers' professional knowledge landscapes.* New York: Teachers College Press.

Clark, C., Moss, P., Goering, S., Herter, R., Lamar, B., Leonard, D., Robbins, S., Russell, M., Templin, M., & Wascha, K. (1996). Collaboration and dialogue: Teachers and researchers engaged in conversation and professional development. *American Educational Research Journal, 33*(1), 193-232.

Clark, C. M. (1995). *Thoughtful teaching.* New York: Teachers College Press.

Clark, R. W. (1992). *Partner schools directory.* Seattle: University of Washington, Center for Educational Renewal.

Cliff, R., Johnson, M., Holland, P., & Veal, M. (1992). Developing the potential for collaborative school leadership. *American Educational Research Journal, 29*(4), 877-908.

Cochran-Smith, M. (1991). Learning to teach against the grain. *Harvard Educational Review, 61*(3), 279-310.

Cohn, M., & Kottkamp, R. (1993). *Teachers: The missing voice in education.* Albany: SUNY Press.

Comer, J. P. (1980). *School power: Implications of an intervention project.* New York: Macmillan.

Comer, J. P., Haynes, N. M., Joyner, E. T., & Ben-Avie, M. (1996). *Rallying the whole village.* New York: Teachers College Press.

Conley, D. T. (1995). *Are you ready to restructure? A guidebook for educators, parents, and community members.* Thousand Oaks, CA: Corwin.

Csikszentmihalyi, M. (1990). *Flow: The psychology of optimal experience.* New York: HarperCollins.

Cunningham, W. C., & Cresso, D. W. (1993). *Cultural leadership: The culture of excellence in education.* Needham Heights, MA: Allyn & Bacon.

Darling-Hammond, L. (1990). Teachers and teaching: Signs of a changing profession. In W. R. Houston (Ed.), *The handbook of research on teacher education* (pp. 267-290). New York: Macmillan.

Darling-Hammond, L. (1993). Reframing the school reform agenda: Developing the capacity for school transformation. *Phi Delta Kappan, 74*(10), 753-761.

Darling-Hammond, L. (1994). *Professional development schools.* New York: Teachers College Press.

Darling-Hammond, L. (1996). The quiet revolution: Rethinking teacher development. *Educational Leadership, 53*(6), 4-10.

Darling-Hammond, L. (1997). *The right to learn: A blueprint for school reform.* San Francisco: Jossey-Bass.

Darling-Hammond, L., & McLaughlin, M. (1995). Policies that support professional development in an era of reform. *Phi Delta Kappan, 76*(8), 597-604.

Deal, T. E., & Kennedy, A. A. (1982). *Corporate cultures: The rites and rituals of corporate life.* Reading, MA: Addison-Wesley.

Deal, T. E., & Peterson, K. D. (1994). *The leadership paradox: Balancing logic and artistry in schools.* San Francisco: Jossey-Bass.

Deming, E. W. (1982). *Out of crisis.* Cambridge: MIT Press.

Dewey, J. (1944). *Democracy and education.* New York: Macmillan. (Original work published in 1916)

Dewey, J. (1960). *How we think.* Chicago: Regnery. (Original work published in 1933)

Dewey, J. (1963). *Experience and education.* New York: Collier. (Original work published in 1938)

Dewey, J. (1975). *Moral principles in education.* Carbondale: Southern Illinois University Press. (Original work published in 1909)

Dewey, J. (1990). *The school and society and the child and the curriculum.* Chicago: University of Chicago Press. (Original work published in 1956)

Dolly, J. P., & Oda, E. A. (1997). Toward a definition of professional development schools. *Peabody Journal of Education, 72*(1), 178-186.

Dorn, R. (1995). The changing roles of principals and staff members. *Wingspan, 10*(2), 7-10.

Doyle, W., & Ponder, G. (1977). The practicality ethic in teacher decision-making. *Interchange, 8*(3), 1-12.

Dreyfus, H. L., & Dreyfus, S. E. (1986). *Mind over machine: The power of human intuition and expertise in the era of the computer.* Oxford: Basil Blackwell.

Duckworth, E. (1996). *"The having of wonderful ideas" and other essays on teaching and learning.* New York: Teachers College Press

Duke, D. (1994). Drift, detachment, and the need for teacher leadership. In D. R. Walling (Ed.), *Teachers as leaders* (pp. 255-273). Bloomington, IN: Phi Delta Kappa.

Edmonds, R. (1979). Effective schools for the urban poor. *Educational Leadership, 37*(1), 15-24.

Eisner, E. W. (1991). What really counts in schools. *Educational Leadership, 48*(5), 10-17.

Eisner, E. W. (1992). Foreword. *If minds matter: A foreword to the future* (Vol. 1, pp. v-vi). Palatine, IL: Skylight. (ERIC Document Reproduction Service No. ED 379 070)

Eisner, E. W. (1993). Why standards may not improve schools. *Educational Leadership, 50* (5), 22-23.

Eisner, E. W. (1994). *The educational imagination: On the design and evaluation of school programs* (3rd ed.). New York: Macmillan.

Elliott, J. (1988, April). *Teachers as researchers: Implications for supervision and teacher education.* Paper presented at the annual meeting of the American Educational Research Association, New Orleans.

Elliott, J. (1991). *Action research for educational change.* Bristol, UK: Taylor & Francis.

Elmore, R. (1995). Getting to scale with good educational practice. *Harvard Educational Review, 66*(1), 1-26.

Elmore, R., Peterson, P., & McCarthey, S. (1996). *Restructuring in the classroom.* San Francisco: Jossey-Bass.

Eraut, M. (1994). *Developing professional knowledge and competence.* London: Falmer.

Erikson, E. H. (1956). The problem of ego identity. *Journal of the American Psychoanalytical Association, 4*(1), 56-121.

Etzioni, A. (1993). *The spirit of community rights, responsibilities, and the communitarian agenda.* New York: Crown.

Evans, R. (1996). *The human side of school change: Reform, resistance, and the real-life problems of innovation.* San Francisco: Jossey-Bass.

Feinburg, M., & Tarrant, J. (1995). *Why smart people do dumb things.* New York: Fireside.

Fine, M. (1991). *Framing dropouts: Notes on the politics of an urban public high school.* Albany: SUNY Press.

Finnan, C., St. John, E. P., McCarthy, J., & Slovacek, S. P. (1996). *Accelerated schools in action: Lessons from the field.* Thousand Oaks, CA: Corwin.

Fosnot, C. T. (Ed.). (1996). *Constructivism: Theory, perspectives, and practice.* New York: Teachers College Press.

Freire, P. (1970). *Pedagogy of the oppressed.* New York: Continuum.

Fried, R. L. (1995). *The passionate teacher.* Boston: Beacon.

Fullan, M. (1991). *The meaning of educational change.* New York: Teachers College Press.

Fullan, M. (1992a). *Successful school improvement.* Philadelphia: Open University Press.

Fullan, M. (1992b). Visions that blind. *Educational Leadership, 49*(5), 19-20.

Fullan, M. (1992c). Why teachers must become change agents. *Educational Leadership, 50*(6), 12-17.

Fullan, M. (1993). *Change forces: Probing the depths of educational reform.* London: Falmer.

Fullan, M. (1994a). Coordinating top-down and bottom-up strategies for educational reform. In R. F. Elmore & S. H. Furhrman (Eds.), *The governance of curriculum: The 1994 yearbook of the Association for Supervision and Curriculum Development.* Alexandria, VA: Association for Supervision and Curriculum Development.

Fullan, M. (1994b). Teacher leadership: A failure to conceptualize. In D. R. Walling (Ed.), *Teachers as leaders: Perspectives on the professional development of teachers* (pp. 241-253). Bloomington, IN: Phi Delta Kappa.

Fullan, M. (1995). Schools as learning organizations: Distant dreams. *Theory into Practice, 34* (4), 230-235.

Fullan, M. (1996a). Leadership for change. In K. Leithwood (Ed.), *International handbook of educational leadership* (pp. 701-722). London: Kluwer.

Fullan, M. (1996b). Turning systemic reform on its head. *Phi Delta Kappan, 77,* 420-423.

Fullan, M. (1997). Emotion and hope: Constructive concepts for complex times. In A. Hargreaves (Ed.), *Positive change for school success: The 1997 Yearbook of the Association for Supervision and Curriculum Development* (pp. 216-233). Alexandria, VA: Association for Supervision and Curriculum Development.

Fullan, M., Galluzzo, G., Morris, P., & Watson, N. (1996). *The rise and stall of reform in teacher education:* New York: The Ford Foundation.

Fullan, M., & Hargreaves, A. (Eds.). (1992). *Teacher development and educational change.* London: Falmer.

Fullan, M., & Hargreaves, A. (1996). *What's worth fighting for in your school?* New York: Teachers College Press.

Fullan, M., & Miles, M. (1992). Getting reform right: What works and what doesn't. *Phi Delta Kappan, 73*(10), 744-752.

Futrell, M. H. (1994). Empowering teachers as learners and leaders. In D. R. Walling (Ed.), *Teachers as leaders: Perspectives on the professional development of teachers* (pp. 19-135). Bloomington, IN: Phi Delta Kappa.

Gardner, H. (1983). *Frames of mind: The theory of multiple intelligences.* New York: Basic Books.

Gardner, H. (1995). *Leading minds.* New York: Basic Books.

Gardner, J. W. (1981). *Self-renewal: The individual and the innovative society* (rev. ed.). New York: Norton.

Gibboney, R. A. (1994). *The stone trumpet: A story of practical school reform, 1960-1990.* Albany: SUNY Press.

Gideonse, H. D. (Ed.). (1992). *Teacher education policy: Narratives, stories and cases.* Albany: SUNY Press.

Glickman, C. D. (1992). The essence of school renewal: The prose has begun. *Educational Leadership, 50*(1), 24-27.

Glickman, C. D. (1993). *Renewing America's schools: A guide for school-based action.* San Francisco: Jossey-Bass.

Glidewell, J. C., Tuckers, S., Todt, M., & Cox, S. (1983). Professional support systems: The teaching profession. In A. Nadler, J. D. Fischer, & B. M. DePaulo (Eds.), *New directions in helping: Allied research in help-seeking and-receiving* (Vol. 3, pp. 198-212). New York: Academic Press.

Goodlad, J. I. (1994a). *Educational renewal: Better teachers, better schools.* San Francisco: Jossey-Bass.

Goodlad, J. I. (1994b). The national network for educational renewal. *Phi Delta Kappan, 75*(8), 632-638.

Goodson, I. F., & Hargreaves, A. (Eds.). (1996). *Teachers' professional lives.* London: Falmer.

Greene, M. (1995). *Releasing the imagination: Essays on education, the arts, and social change.* San Francisco: Jossey-Bass.

Griffin, G. (1996, April). *Restructuring schools: Implications for teacher education.* Paper presented at the annual meeting of the American Educational Research Association, New York.

Grimmett, P. P., & Crehan, E. P. (1992). The nature of collegiality in teacher development: The case of clinical supervision. In M. Fullan & A. Hargreaves (Eds.), *Teacher development and educational change* (pp. 56-85). London: Falmer.

Hachman, J. R., Oldham, G., Johnson, R., & Purdy, K. (1975). A new strategy for job enhancement. *California Management Review, 17*(4), 57-76.

Hare, W. (1979). *Open-mindedness and education.* Kingston & Montreal: McGill-Queen's University Press.

Hare, W. (1993a). *Attitudes in teaching and education.* Calgary: Detselig.

Hare, W. (1993b). *What makes a good teacher: Reflections on some characteristics central to the educational enterprise.* London, Ontario: Althouse.

Hargreaves, A. (1994). *Changing teachers, changing times: Teachers' work and culture in the postmodern age.* New York: Teachers College Press.

Hargreaves, A., & Dawe, R. (1990). Paths of professional development: Contrived collegiality, collaborative culture, and the case of peer coaching. *Teaching & Teacher Education, 6*(3), 227-241.

Hargreaves, A., & Fullan, M. (1992). *Understanding teacher development.* New York: Teachers College Press.

Hargreaves, A., & Fullan, M. (1997). *What's worth fighting for out there.* New York: Teachers College Press.

Harris, P. (1992). Restructuring for learning. In A. L. Costa, J. Belanca, & R. Fogarty (Eds.), *If minds matter: A foreword to the future* (Vol. 1, pp. 3-11). Palatine, IL: Skylight. (ERIC Document Reproduction Service No. ED 379 070)

Hawley, W. (1994). *Revisioning the education of teachers.* San Francisco: Jossey-Bass.

Hawley, W. D., & Rosenholtz, S. J, with Goodstein, H. L., & Hasselbring, T. (1984). Good schools: What research says about improving student achievement [special issue]. *Peabody Journal of Education, 61*(4), 1-178.

Herzberg, F., Mausner, B., & Snyderman, B. (1959). *The motivation to work.* New York: John Wiley.

Holmes Group, Inc. (1990). *Tomorrow's schools: Principles for the design of professional development schools.* East Lansing, MI: Author.

Hubberman, M. (1988). Teachers' careers and school improvement. *Journal of Curriculum Studies, 20*(2), 119-132.

Isaacson, N., & Bamburg, J. (1992). Can schools become learning organizations? *Educational Leadership, 50*(3), 42-44.

Jackson, P. W. (1986). *The practice of teaching.* New York: Teachers College Press.

Jackson, P. W. (1992). *Untaught lessons.* New York: Teachers College Press.

Johnson, S. M. (1990). *Teachers at work: Achieving success in schools.* New York: Basic Books.

Jones, M. G., & Vesilind, E. M. (1996). Putting practice into theory: Changes in the organization of preservice teachers' pedagogical knowledge. *American Educational Research Journal, 33*(1), 91-118.

Joyce, B., Wolf, J., & Calhoun, E. (1993). *The self-renewing school.* Alexandria, VA: Association for Supervision and Curriculum Development.

Kaplan, J., & Edelfelt, R. A. (Eds.). (1996). *Teachers for the new millennium: Aligning teacher development, national goals, and high standards for all students.* Thousand Oaks, CA: Corwin.

Kegan, R. (1992). *The evolving self: Problems and process in human development.* Cambridge, MA: Harvard University Press.

Kent, K., & Abbey, T. (1995). Collaborative work cultures, learning communities and school change. *Cooperative Learning,* 15(1), 21-25.

Kompf, M., Bond, W. R., Dworet, D., & Boak, R. T. (Eds.). (1996). *Changing research and practice: Teachers' professionalism, identities and knowledge.* London: Falmer.

LaBoskey, V. K. (1994). *Development of reflective practice: A study of preservice teachers.* New York: Teachers College Press.

Ladd, H. F. (Ed.). (1996). *Holding schools accountable: Performance-based reform in education.* Washington, DC: Brookings Institution Press.

Lambert, L. (1988). Staff development redesigned. *Phi Delta Kappan, 69*(9), 665-668.

Lambert, L. (1989). The end of an era of staff development. *Educational Leadership, 45*(7), 78-83.

Lambert, L., Colay, M., Dietz, M. E., Kent, K., & Richert, A. E. (1997). *Who will save our schools? Teachers as constructivist leaders.* Thousand Oaks, CA: Corwin.

Lambert, L., Walker, D., Zimmerman, D., Cooper, J., Lambert, M., Gardner, M., & Ford-Slack, P. J. (Eds.). (1995). *The constructivist leader.* New York: Teachers College Press.

Leithwood, K. A. (1992). The principal's role in teacher development. In M. Fullan & A. Hargreaves (Eds.), *Teacher development and educational change.* London: Falmer.

Lemming, J. S. (1994). Character education and the creation of community. *The Responsive Community, 4*(4), 49-57.

Levine, M. (Ed.). (1992). *Professional practice schools: Linking teacher education and school reform.* New York: Teachers College Press.

Levine, M., & Trauchtman, B. (Eds.). (1997). *Building professional development schools: Politics, practice and policy.* New York: Teachers College Press.

Lewin, K. (1951). *Field theory in social science.* New York: Harper & Row.

Lewin, K. (1964). Resolving social conflicts. In W. Bennis, E. Schein, & D. Berlew (Eds.), *Interpersonal dynamics: Essays and readings on human interactions.* (pp. 60-65). Homewood, IL: Dorsey.

Lichtenstein, G., McLaughlin, M., & Knudsen, J. (1992). Teacher empowerment and professional knowledge. In A. Lieberman (Ed.), *The changing context of teaching: Ninety-first yearbook of the National Society for the Study of Education* (pp. 37-58). Chicago: University of Chicago Press.

Lieberman, A. (1989). *Building a professional culture in schools.* New York: Teachers College Press.

Lieberman, A. (1995a). Practices that support teacher development: Transforming conceptions of professional learning. *Phi Delta Kappan, 76*(8), 591-596.

Lieberman, A. (Ed.). (1995b). *Professional development in the reform era.* New York: Teachers College Press.

Lieberman, A., & Miller, L. (1986). School improvement: Themes and variations. In A. Lieberman (Ed.), *Rethinking school improvement: Research craft and concept.* New York: Teachers College Press.

Lieberman, A., & Miller, L. (1990a). Restructuring schools: What matters and what works. *Phi Delta Kappan, 71*(10), 759-764.

Lieberman, A., & Miller, L. (1990ba). The social realities of teaching. In A. Lieberman (Ed.), *Schools as collaborative cultures: Creating the future now* (pp. 153-163). London: Falmer.

Lighthall, F. (1973). Multiple realities and organizational nonsolutions: An essay on anatomy of educational innovation. *School Review, 81*(2), 255-293.

Little, J. W. (1982). Norms of collegiality and experimentation: Workplace conditions of school success. *AERA Journal, 19*(3), 325-340.

Little, J. W. (1987). Teachers as colleagues. In V. R. Koehler (Ed.), *Educators' handbook: A research perspective* (pp. 491-518). New York: Longman.

Little, J. W. (1990). Teachers as colleagues. In A. Lieberman (Ed.), *Schools as collaborative cultures: Creating the future now* (pp. 165-193). London: Falmer.

Little, J. W. (1992). Teacher development and educational policy. In M. Fullan & A. Hargreaves (Eds.), *Teacher development and educational change* (pp. 170-193). London: Falmer.

Little, J. W. (1993). Teachers' professional development in a climate of educational reform. *Educational Evaluation and Policy Analysis, 15*(2), 129-151.

Little, J. W., Gerritz, W. H., Stern, D. S., Guthrie, J. W., Kirst, M. W., & March, D. D. (1987). *Staff development in California: Public and personal investments, program patterns, and policy choices.* San Francisco: Far West Laboratory for Educational Research and Development.

Lord, T. R. (1994). Using constructivism to enhance student learning in college biology. *Journal of College Science Teaching, 23*(6), 346-348.

Lortie, D. (1975). *School teacher: A sociological study.* Chicago: University of Chicago Press.

Loughran, J. (1996). *Developing reflective practice: Learning about teaching and learning through modeling.* London: Falmer.

Loughran, J., & Northfield, J. (1996). *Opening the classroom door: Teacher, researcher, learner.* London: Falmer.

Loughran, J., & Russell, T. (Eds.). (1997). *Teaching about teaching: Purpose, passion and pedagogy in teacher education.* London: Falmer.

Louis, K. S., & Kruse, S. (1995). *Professionalism and community.* Thousand Oaks, CA: Corwin.

Louis, K. S., & Miles, K. B. (1990). *Improving the urban high school: What works and why.* New York: Teachers College Press.

MacDonald, J. (1996). *Redesigning school: Lessons for the 21st century.* San Francisco: Jossey-Bass.

MacIntyre, A. (1984). *After virtue: A study in moral theory.* Notre Dame, IN: University of Notre Dame Press.

MacKinnon, A. M., & Scarff-Seatter, C. (1997). Constructivism: Contradictions and confusions in teacher education. In V. Richardson (Ed.), *Constructivist teacher education: Building a world of new understanding* (pp. 38-55). London: Falmer.

McLaughlin, M., & Talbert, J. E. (1993). *Contexts that matter for teaching and learning.* Stanford, CA: Stanford University, Center for Research as the Context of Secondary School Teaching.

McNamara, D., & Desforges, C. (1979). Professional studies as a source of theory. In R. J. Alexander & E. Wormald (Eds.), *Professional studies for teaching* (pp. 46-60). Guildford: SRHE.

Meier, D. (1992). Reinventing teaching. *Teachers College Record, 93*(4), 594-609.

Meier, D. (1997a). How our schools could be: Standard, top-down mandates and grass-roots communities. *Rethinking Schools, 11*(4), 8-9.

Meier, D. (1997b). *Transforming public education.* New York: Teachers College Press.

Mill, J. (1965). *On liberty.* Indianapolis, IN: Bobbs-Merill. (Original work published in 1859)

Muncey, D. E., & McQuillan, P. J. (1996). *Reform and resistance in schools and classrooms: An ethnographic view of the coalition of essential schools.* New Haven, CT: Yale University Press.

Murgatroyd, S., & Morgan, C. (1993). *Total quality management and the school.* Philadelphia, PA: Open University Press.

Murphy, J. (1991). *Restructuring schools.* New York: Teachers College Press.

Murphy, J. (1992). *The landscape of leadership preparation.* Newbury Park, CA: Corwin.

Murphy, J., & Beck, L. G. (1995). *School-based management as school reform: Taking stock.* Thousand Oaks, CA: Corwin.

Murphy, J., & Beck, L. G. (1996). *The four imperatives of a successful school.* Thousand Oaks, CA: Corwin.

Murphy, J., & Hallinger, P. (Eds.) (1993). *Restructuring schooling: Learning from ongoing efforts.* Thousand Oaks, CA: Corwin.

Murphy, J., & Louis, K. S. (Eds.). (1994). *Reshaping the principalship: Insights from transformational reform efforts.* Thousand Oaks, CA: Corwin.

Myers, C. B. (1979). Diffusion does not equal instructional change. *Social Education, 43*(6), 485-489.

Myers, C. B. (1981). The disseminator's bias and instructional change. *Counterpoint, 2*(1), 15-16. (ERIC Document Reproduction Service No. ED 156 546)

Myers, C. B. (1995a, April). *Building and sustaining school-university collaborative learning communities: Overcoming potential inhibiting factors.* Paper presented at the annual meeting of the American Association of Colleges for Teacher Education, Washington, DC.

Myers, C. B. (1995b, April). *The importance of self-study in teacher education reform and re-accreditation efforts.* Paper presented at the annual meeting of the American Educational Research Association, San Francisco.

Myers, C. B. (1996a, April). *Beyond the PDS: Schools as professional learning communities: A proposal based on an analysis of PDS efforts of the 1990s.* Paper presented at the annual meeting of the American Education Research Association, New York. (ERIC Document Reproduction Service No. ED 400 227)

Myers, C. B. (1996b, April). *University-school collaborations: A need to reconceptualize schools as professional learning communities instead of partnerships.* Paper presented at the annual meeting of the American Educational Research Association, New York. (ERIC Document Reproduction Service No. ED 400 228)

Myers, C. B. (1997a, March). *The absence of self-study in school-university teacher education reform.* Paper presented at the annual meeting of the American Educational Research Association, Chicago.

Myers, C. B. (1997b, March). *Reconceptualizing learning, teaching, and schools as the next stage in teacher education reform and school renewal.* Paper presented at the annual meeting of the American Educational Research Association, Chicago.

Myers, C. B., & Myers, L. K. (1995). *The professional educator: A new introduction to teaching and schools.* Belmont, CA: Wadsworth.

Nadler, N. M. (1986). Organizations as learning communities: How managers and front line supervisors learn in nonformal ways. Unpublished doctoral dissertation, George Washington University.

Newmann, F., & Wehlage, G. G. (1995). *Successful school restructuring.* Madison: University of Wisconsin, Center on Organization and Restructuring of Schools.

Noddings, N. (1992). *The challenge to care in schools.* New York: Teachers College Press.

Noddings, N. (1996). On community. *Educational Theory, 46*(3), 245-267.

Oakeshott, M. (1962). *Rationalism in politics: And other essays.* London: Methuen.

Oakeshott, M. (1975). *On human conduct.* Oxford: Clarendon.

O'Neil, J. (1995). On schools as learning organizations: A conversation with Peter Senge. *Educational Leadership, 52*(7), 20-23.

Osguthorpe, R. T., Harris, R. C., Harris, M. F., & Black, S. (Eds.). (1995). *Partner schools: Centers for educational renewal.* San Francisco: Jossey-Bass.

Peters, T. J., & Waterman, R. H., Jr. (1982). *In search of excellence.* New York: Warner.

Peterson, P. L., McCarthey, S. J., & Elmore, R. E. (1996). Learning from school restructuring. *American Educational Research Journal, 33*(1), 119-154.

Petrie, H. G. (Ed.). (1995). *Professionalism, partnership, and power: Building professional development schools.* Albany: SUNY Press.

Piaget, J. (1950). *The psychology of intelligence.* London: Routledge & Paul.

Pipho, C. (1992). A decade of education reform. *Phi Delta Kappan, 74*(4), 278-279.

Polanyi, M. (1966). *The tacit dimension.* New York: Doubleday.

Polanyi, M. (1969). *Knowing and being.* Chicago: University of Chicago Press.

Poplin, M. (1993). *Voices from the inside.* Claremont, CA: Claremont Graduate School, Institute for Education in Transformation.

Prawat, R. S. (1992). From individual differences to learning communities—Our changing focus. *Educational Leadership, 49*(7), 9-13.

Prawat, R. S. (1993). The role of the principal in the development of learning communities. *Wingspan, 9*(2), 7-9.

Richardson, V. (Ed.). (1997). *Constructivist teacher education: Building a world of new understanding.* London: Falmer.

Richert, A. E. (1994, April). *The culture of inquiry and the challenge of change: Teacher learning and the school change context.* Paper presented at the Spencer Foundation Fellows Forum, New Orleans, LA.

Rosenholtz, S. (1989). *Teachers' workplace: The social organization of schools.* White Plains, NY: Longman.

Ross, W. W., Cornett, J. W., & McCutcheon, G. (Eds.). (1992). *Teacher personal theorizing: Connecting curriculum practice, theory, and research.* Albany: SUNY Press.

Russell, T. (1997). Teaching teachers: How I teach is the message. In J. Loughran & R. Russell (Eds.),*Teaching about teaching: Purpose, passion, and pedagogy in teacher education* (Ch. 3). London: Falmer.

Russell, T., & Korthagen, F. (Eds.). (1995). *Teachers who teach teachers: Reflections on teacher education.* London: Falmer.

Ryle, G. (1949). *The concept of mind.* London: Hutchinson.

Saphier, J., & D'Auria, J. (1993). *How to bring vision to school improvement through core outcomes, commitments, and beliefs.* Carlisle, MA: Research for Better Teaching.

Sarason, S. B. (1990). *The predictable failure of educational reform: Can we change course before it's too late?* San Francisco: Jossey-Bass.

Sarason, S. B. (1993). *The case for change: Rethinking the preparation of educators.* San Francisco: Jossey-Bass.

Sarason, S. B. (1995). Some reactions to what we have learned. *Phi Delta Kappan, 77*(1), 84-85.

Sarason, S. B. (1996). *Revisiting "the culture of the school and the problem of change."* New York: Teachers College Press.

Sarason, S. B. (1997). *How schools might be governed and why.* New York: Teachers College Press.

Schaefer, R. J. (1967). *The school as a center of inquiry.* New York: HarperCollins.

Scherer, M. (1994). On schools where students want to be: A conversation with D. Meier. *Educational Leadership, 52*(1), 4-8.

Schlechty, P. C. (1990). *Schools for the 21st century: Leadership imperatives for educational reform.* San Francisco: Jossey-Bass.

Schön, D. A. (1983). *The reflective practitioner: How professionals think in action.* New York: Basic Books.

Schön, D. A. (1987). *Educating the reflective practitioner: Toward a new design for teaching and learning in the professions.* San Francisco: Jossey-Bass.

Schwab, J. J. (1962). The concept of structure of a discipline. *Educational Record, 43*(3), 197-205.

Schwab, J. J. (1978). *Science, curriculum, and liberal education.* Chicago: University of Chicago Press.

Senge, P. M. (1990). *The fifth discipline: The art and practice of the learning organization.* New York: Doubleday.

Sergiovanni, T. J. (1992). *Moral leadership: Getting to the heart of school improvement.* San Francisco: Jossey-Bass.

Sergiovanni, T. J. (1994). *Building community in schools.* San Francisco: Jossey-Bass.

Sergiovanni, T. J. (1995). *The principalship: A reflective practice perspective* (3rd ed.). Needham Heights, MA: Allyn & Bacon.

Sergiovanni, T. J. (1996). *Leadership for the schoolhouse: How is it different? Why is it important?* San Francisco: Jossey-Bass.

Sergiovanni, T. J., & Moore, J. H. (1989). *Schooling for tomorrow: Directing reforms to issues that count.* Needham Heights, MA: Allyn & Bacon.

Shanker, A. (1990). Staff development and the restructured school. In B. Joyce (Ed.), *Changing school culture through staff development* (pp. 91-103). Alexandria, VA: Association for Supervision and Curriculum Development.

Shedd, J. B., & Bacharach, S. B. (1991). *Tangled hierarchies: Teachers as professionals and the management of schools.* San Francisco: Jossey-Bass.

Shulman, L. S. (1986). Those who understand: Knowledge growth in teaching. *Educational Researcher, 15*(2), 4-14.

Shulman, L. S. (1989). Teaching alone, teaching together: Needed agendas for the new reforms. In T. J. Sergiovanni & H. H. Moore (Eds.), *Schooling for tomorrow: Directing reforms to issues that count* (pp. 166-187). Needham Heights, MA: Allyn & Bacon.

Siegel, J. (1997). *Rationality redeemed? Future dialogues on an educational ideal.* New York: Routledge.

Sikes, P. J. (1992). Imposed change and the experienced teacher. In M. Fullan & A. Hargreaves (Eds.), *Teacher development and educational change* (pp. 36-55). London: Falmer.

Simpson, D., & Jackson, M. (1984). *The teacher as philosopher: A primer in philosophy of education.* Toronto: Methuen.

Simpson, D., & Jackson, M. (1997). *Educational reform: A Deweyan perspective.* New York: Garland.

Sirotnik, K. A. (1989). The school as the center of change. In T. J. Sergiovanni & J. H. Moore (Eds.), *Schooling for tomorrow: Directing reforms to issues that count* (pp. 89-113). Needham Heights, MA: Allyn & Bacon.

Slater, J. J. (1996). *Anatomy of a collaboration: Study of a college of education/public school partnership.* New York: Garland.

Strike, K., & Soltis, J. (1992). *The ethics of teaching* (2nd ed.). New York: Teachers College Press.

Sykes, G. (1996). Reform *of* and *as* professional development. *Phi Delta Kappan, 78,* 465-467.

Taba, H. (1962). *Curriculum development: Theory and practice.* New York: Harcourt, Brace and World.

Tabachnich, B. R., & Zeichner, K. (Eds.). (1991). *Issues and practices in inquiry oriented teacher education.* London: Falmer.

Teitel, L., & Del Prete, T. (1995). *Creating PDS partnerships: A resource guide.* Boston: University of Massachusetts, Massachusetts Field Center for Teaching and Learning.

Tillich, P. (1952). *The courage to be.* New Haven, CT: Yale University Press.

Tom, A. (1980). The reform of teacher education through research: A futile quest. *Teachers College Record, 82*(1), 15-29.

Tönnies, F. (1957). *Gemeinschaft und gesellschaft* [Community and society] (C. P. Loomis, Ed. & Trans.). New York: HarperCollins. (Original work published in 1887)

Van Manen, M. (1991). *The tact of teaching; The meaning of pedagogical thoughtfulness.* Albany: SUNY Press.

Vygotsky, L. (1962). *Thought and language.* Boston: MIT Press.

Vygotsky, L. (1978). *Mind in society.* Cambridge, MA: Harvard University Press.

Warren, T. (Ed.). (1996). *Partnerships in teacher education: Schools and colleges working together.* Lanham, MD: University Press of America.

Wasley, P. A. (1993). *Teachers who lead: Rhetoric and reform and the realities of practice.* New York: Teachers College Press.

Wehlage, G., Rutter, R., Smith, G., Lesko, H., & Fernandez, R. (1990). *Reducing the risk: Schools as communities of support.* Philadelphia: Falmer.

Weick, K. (1976). Educational organizations as loosely coupled systems. *Administrative Science Quarterly, 21*(2), 1-19.

Weiss, C. H. (1993). Shared decision making about what? A comparison of schools with and without teacher participation. *Teachers College Record, 95*(1), 69-92.

Weiss, C. H. (1995). The four "I's" of school reform: How interests, ide-
    ology, information, and institution affect teachers and principals.
    Harvard Educational Review, 65(4), 571-592.
Wells, C., & Wells, G. (1992). *Constructing knowledge together: Class-
    rooms as centers of inquiry and literacy.* Portsmouth, NH: Heine-
    mann.
Wheatley, G. H. (1991). Constructivist perspectives on science and
    mathematics learning. *Science Education, 75*(1), 9-21.
Wheatley, M. J. (1992). *Leadership and the new science.* San Fran-
    cisco, CA: Berrett-Koehler.
Yager, R. (1993). The constructivist learning model: Toward real reform
    in science education. *The Science Teacher, 60*(1), 53-57.
Zeichner, K. M., & Liston, D. P. (1996) *Reflective teaching: An introduc-
    tion.* Mahwah, NJ: Lawrence Erlbaum.

Index

CORWIN
PRESS

The Corwin Press logo—a raven striding across an open book—
represents the happy union of courage and learning. We are a
professional-level publisher of books and journals for K–12 educators,
and we are committed to creating and providing resources that embody these qualities. Corwin's motto is "Success for All Learners."

The Rising of the Shield Hero 5

Aneko Yusagi

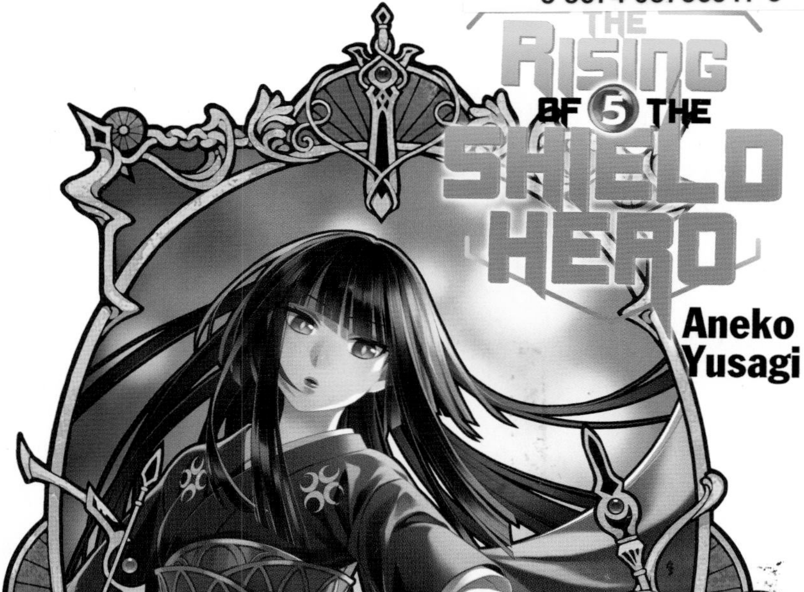

Glass

Itsuki Kawasumi

L'Arc Berg

Therese

"L'Arc, calm down, will you?"

"I know, I know! But I can't help it. Ships get me so excited."

Sigh. This guy sounded like he had the maturity of a kindergartener.

Apparently hearing my sigh, he spun on his heels and faced me.

"What's the matter, kiddo?"